Happy Cooking!

Norman & Jenny

COOL FOOD

COOL FOOD

Delicious dishes to serve chilled or
at room temperature

NATHALIE HAMBRO

Conran Octopus

To José
To Alfred

This edition published 1988 by
Conran Octopus Limited
37 Shelton Street
London WC2H 9HN

Editors Vicky Hayward, Catherine Carpenter
Art Editor Caroline Langton
Photographer Paul Bussell
Photographic Art Direction Valerie Wright Heneghan
Home Economist Berit Vinegrad
Photographic Stylist Penny Mishcon

ISBN 1 85029 108 X

*The publishers would like to thank the following
for their assistance with props:*
Heal's, 196 Tottenham Court Road, London W1;
The Conran Shop, 77–79 Fulham Road, London SW3..

Previous page: Kumquat Compôte and Strawberries with Claret

Typeset by Vantage Typesetters Limited
Printed and bound in Hong Kong

CONTENTS

INTRODUCTION

Many top chefs now recommend eating all sorts of dishes at room temperature, because the flavours and texture of the food are at their best that way. As well as being *à la mode*, the advantage of cool food is, of course, that it can be prepared in advance – a tremendous help when faced with a busy day or a large number of people. In what seems to me to be an increasingly rushed world, I firmly believe in a practical approach to cooking and not being a slave to the cooker and clock, but I also believe that eating at home with friends is one of the great pleasures in life. So I have devised all the recipes in this book for food which can be prepared, with little fuss, either ahead of time, or quickly and easily at the last moment. None rely on precise timing so they allow you to eat when you want to, rather than when the food dictates.

I like to serve a cluster of dishes – rather than a set menu with a starter and main course – so that people can help themselves to varying amounts of different dishes. For this reason the recipes are grouped into categories of food, like Eggs, Cheese and Grains, and although I offer suggestions of which dishes you might serve together, you must feel free to experiment yourself. One of the delights of cooking is the discovery of new combinations of flavours, not only through putting together different dishes, but also by being flexible with the ingredients too. A number of my recipes were spontaneous creations, sometimes the result of access to limited ingredients which can force one to be more inventive and original, and sometimes inspired by what looked most interesting in the market and shops.

One of the most important aspects of cooking for me is to use the freshest possible ingredients; and I also avoid over-refined foods and all those which use too much cooked fat. We should all take care of our guests' health as well as our own. I think that the appearance of food is also important and in all my recipes I have thought about combinations of colour as well as of taste and texture. I like to present food as imaginatively as possible, and it is always worth taking just an extra minute or two to make a dish visually more appealing, because it is the sight as well as the smell of good food that stimulates the taste buds.

I hope that using this book will give you more time to relax and enjoy your guests – which is the most important thing of all, as much of the success of any meal depends upon the host or hostess being relaxed and welcoming. *Bon appétit.*

Nathalie Hambro

Rigatoni, Smoked Chicken and Mango

Here the pasta is made Indian-style with curry and chutney. The sweet and sour combination gives this dish an unusual flavour. Rigatoni is a wide-ribbed tubular pasta about 1 in (2.5 cm) long. It goes well with Radicchio, Bean Shoot and Mint Salad, p.79, or Squash and Radish Salad, p.74, or with mange-touts steamed for 3 minutes and refreshed with cold water.

---

1 lb (500 g) rigatoni

½ pt/10 fl oz (300 ml) sour cream

½ teaspoon **curry paste**

½ lb (250 g) boned smoked chicken

3 pieces mango chutney, sliced

salt and freshly ground black pepper

4 thin spring onions

● Fill a large saucepan three-quarters full with salted water and bring to the boil. Cook the pasta for 10 to 12 minutes. Drain.
● In a large bowl beat together the sour cream and curry paste. Add the smoked chicken (cut into medium-sized pieces) and chutney slices. Toss in the rigatoni and season to taste. Add spring onions, cut across at a slant. Let cool and serve either at room temperature or chilled.

Serves 6

Green Tortellini with Olives and Lemon Grass

Try to buy herbed black olives rather than those in brine. Also, it is important to use fresh lemon grass, which has a very distinctive flavour. Dried lemon grass will not do. Fresh tortellini are available in most supermarkets with ricotta and spinach filling. This dish can be served with Yellow Peppers with Spinach, p.91, or Okra and Coconut, p.83. It also makes a nice accompaniment for poultry or game.

---

18 oz (250 g) packet green tortellini

4 tablespoons fruity olive oil

½ lb (250 g) black olives, stoned and cut in two

1 root fresh lemon grass, thinly sliced

salt and freshly ground black pepper

● Cook the tortellini for 10–12 minutes in a saucepan filled with boiling salted water and a teaspoon of oil. Drain well. In a bowl, toss the tortellini with the olive oil, black olives and lemon grass. Cool to room temperature and season to taste.

Serves 4–6

Top: *Rigatoni, Smoked Chicken and Mango*
Bottom: *Green Tortellini with Olives and Lemon Grass*

Mozzarella and Ricotta Salad with Anchovies

It is important here that you use very fresh cheese and, if possible, fresh green peppercorns, as their fragrance is better than that of dried ones. But avoid at all costs the peppercorns in brine. This is excellent served with steamed fish and Farfalle with Broccoli and Pine Nuts, p. 26.

---

2 whole mozzarella cheeses

½ lb (250 g) ricotta cheese

3 tablespoons fruity olive oil

2–3 sprigs fresh green peppercorns

6–8 anchovy fillets

● Slice the mozzarella and ricotta cheeses neatly and place them overlapping on a flattish dish. Sprinkle all over with olive oil. Scatter the fresh green peppercorns, lightly crushed, over the top. Place the anchovy fillets, cut in half lengthways, at random on top.
● Serve without delay.

Serves 4–6

Rice and Parmesan Salad

For a more substantial salad you may add half a cucumber or two courgettes, either of them chopped. It is important to use the best, freshest Parmesan, so it is worthwhile buying it from a good Italian grocer. This makes an excellent accompaniment to Steamed Chicken Balls, p. 54, or Turkey Rolls, p. 60.

---

8 oz (250 g) patna rice

1 tablespoon fruity olive oil

½ pt/10 fl oz (300 ml) sour cream or Greek yoghurt

2 oz (50 g) Parmesan cheese, freshly grated

about 6 sprigs fresh tarragon

celery salt and freshly ground black pepper

● Cook the rice in boiling salted water until just tender. Drain and rinse well. While the rice is still warm, toss it in a bowl with the olive oil. Reserve.
● In another bowl, beat together the sour cream (or Greek yoghurt) with the Parmesan and whole tarragon leaves stripped off the stems. Season sparingly with the celery salt, taking the Parmesan's saltiness into account, and pepper to taste. Toss in the rice and serve at room temperature.

Serves 6

Variation: Replace the tarragon with six to eight fresh sage leaves, finely shredded.

Top: *Rice and Parmesan Salad*
Bottom: *Mozzarella and Ricotta Salad with Anchovies*

Scrambled Eggs with Radicchio

The cold scrambled eggs are piled in a little mound inside the cup-shaped radicchio leaf. Serve with a crunchy dish such as Cauliflower with Yoghurt and Oregano, p.71, or Broad Beans and Baby Carrots with Savory, p.64.

---

2 oz (60 g) butter

8 large eggs

salt and freshly ground black pepper

1 tablespoon chopped chives

6 large radicchio leaves

1 × 3½ oz (100 g) jar of salmon roe

● In a heavy saucepan melt the butter until it reaches the 'noisette' stage, i.e. when a nutty aroma escapes from the pan. Reduce the heat and immediately pour in the lightly beaten eggs, seasoned with salt and freshly ground black pepper. Stir constantly with a wooden spoon until the eggs are evenly set but not firm. Add some of the finely chopped chives and transfer immediately to a soup plate. Allow to cool.

● Just before serving place the radicchio leaves on a flat dish or basket. Pile some of the egg mixture in each 'cup', spoon a little salmon roe on top and scatter on the remaining chives.

Serves 4 to 6

Variation: Replace the salmon roe with a few truffle shavings.

From left to right: *Quails' Eggs en Gelée (p.14), Scrambled Eggs with Radicchio, Stilton and Pecan Bites (p.14)*

Quail's Eggs en Gelée

The traditional recipe for this main dish uses standard size eggs but the aspic is sufficient for three small quail's eggs. Unlike seagull's eggs, which are sold already prepared, quail's eggs need cooking. They go well with either Mushroom Bread, p.15, or Coconut and Orange Muffins, p.124, and Rice and Parmesan Salad, p.11.

---

12 quail's eggs

4 spinach leaves

1 pt (600 ml) well-flavoured chicken stock

1 sachet (about ½ oz/12 g) gelatine

allspice

salt and freshly ground black pepper

● Cook the eggs for precisely 3 minutes and cool under cold running water. Peel and reserve. Clean the spinach leaves thoroughly, removing the stems. Steam for 1 minute and refresh immediately in chilled water. Drain and pat dry.
● Heat the stock, sprinkle over the gelatine and stir until completely dissolved. Let cool.
● Meanwhile chill 4 moulds, such as dariole moulds or ramekins. Then line the bottoms and sides with some aspic, swirling it all around. Press a spinach leaf flat in each mould. Use 3 eggs per mould and season with allspice, salt and pepper. Fill with the remaining aspic and refrigerate for at least 4 hours or until set.
● Just before serving, run a blade around the sides of each mould and invert on a serving dish, giving a shake to displace the aspic. Unmould neatly.

Serves 2–4

Stilton and Pecan Bites

These bite-size cheese and nut balls are attractively wrapped in a dill spray. If you find Stilton too strong, replace it with Gorganzola or Cambozola cheese. Serve with croûtons or thin biscuits as an appetizer or snack or with steamed watercress and Chicken in Lemon and Tomato Aspic, p.62, as a main course.

½ lb (250 g) Stilton cheese

1 oz (25 g) butter, at room temperature

½ teaspoon caraway seeds

2 oz (60 g) pecan nuts, chopped

a few fresh dill sprays

● In a bowl, mash the cheese, butter, caraway seeds and pecan nuts. Refrigerate for at least 1 hour or until firm. Form into balls the size of a small walnut and press a dill spray around each one.

Makes about 12

Mushroom Bread

This unusual wholemeal bread is flavoured with Italian dried mushrooms combined with cumin seeds, which give it a woody, earthy flavour. It is easier to use a dried yeast which you blend directly with the flour, thus saving time by eliminating the preliminary stage of fermentation in water. Serve with any egg or cheese dish.

---

3 oz (85 g) dried mushrooms

½ pt (300 ml) warm water

12 oz (340 g) wholemeal flour

4 oz (125 g) strong white flour

1 packet Easy Blend dried yeast

1 teaspoon cumin seeds

1 teaspoon sea salt

2 tablespoons fruity olive oil

● Soak the dried mushrooms for 1 hour in the warm water. Squeeze dry, reserving the liquid, and chop into small pieces. In a large bowl, sift together the wholemeal flour, white flour, yeast, cumin seeds and salt. Stir the olive oil into the mushroom water. Make a well in the centre of the bowl and gradually pour the liquid mixture over the dry ingredients, incorporating it roughly with a wooden spoon. When the dough becomes too stiff and sticky to work, turn it onto a floured board and knead for 8 to 10 minutes or until the dough is smooth and pliable. Halfway through the kneading, add the chopped mushrooms. Shape the dough into a ball, pat it all over with oil and place in a 1 lb (500 g) greased bread tin. Cover, set in a warm place and leave to rise for about 1¼ hours or until nearly doubled in bulk.
● Preheat the oven to 350°F/180°C/Gas 4.
● Bake the bread for 45 minutes. The loaf should sound hollow when removed from the tin and tapped on the bottom with your knuckles. Leave to cool on a rack.

Makes 1 loaf

Fromage de Celeri

A fresh-tasting dish to serve with a nutty wholemeal bread and plenty of good butter. As the ricotta's lovely fresh taste doesn't last, this dish should be eaten within a day. I serve this with Saffron or Mushroom Bread, p.17 and 15, and Potato, Turnip and Radicchio Salad, p.67. The Smoked Duck and Prunes, p.54, also complements this dish.

1½ lb (750 g) ricotta cheese

1 tablespoon sour cream

1 celery heart, finely chopped

2 heaped tablespoons chopped chives

salt and freshly ground black pepper

● With a large fork mash the ricotta and sour cream, then add the celery and chives. Season to taste. Press the mixture quite hard into an attractive container like a jelly mould or other textured bowl. Refrigerate for 1 hour and unmould, which should be very easy, on a serving dish.

Serves 6

Saffron Bread

This is a delicious, light bread with a lovely golden crust and a rich ochre colour inside. It is also nice toasted. Serve with a soup or a fish dish, or with Fromage de Celeri, p.15.

2 teaspoons dried yeast

4 tablespoons tepid water

½ pt (300 ml) milk

about 10 saffron stigmas

2 lb (1 kg) strong white flour

2 teaspoons salt

4 eggs, beaten

- Sprinkle the yeast over the water and leave for about 10 minutes or until frothy. Meanwhile heat the milk and saffron to boiling point, then leave to cool until lukewarm. Put the flour and salt in a large bowl, make a well in the centre and pour in the yeast mixture, stirring lightly. Add the saffron, milk and eggs. With a wooden spoon, mix in well, adding more milk if the dough becomes too stiff. Turn out on a floured surface and knead for 4 to 5 minutes or until the dough is elastic but no longer sticky. Return to the bowl, cover with a plastic bag and leave to rise for about 1 hour.
- Grease 2 × 1 lb (500 g) bread tins. Punch down the dough, with your fist, to its initial volume and knead once more for 4 to 6 minutes. Divide the dough in two and push it into the prepared tins. Invert and replace, upside down, in the tins, so that the greased bottom is on top. Cover with the polythene bag and leave to rise, for a second time, for about 1 hour.
- Preheat the oven to 375°F/190°C/Gas 5.
- Bake for 30 minutes. Remove the loaves from the tins and leave them to cool on a rack.

Makes 2 loaves.

From left to right: *Mushroom Bread (p.15), Saffron Bread, Fromage de Celeri (p.15)*

Couscous and Vegetable Mould

You can vary the combination of vegetables for this recipe, but green ones work best. I shape the couscous mixture into individual dariole moulds or small bowls, but you can also use a large savarin or charlotte mould. Serve with Tomato and Parsley Sauce, p.20. Accompany this dish with Citrons Confits, p.80, and Mussel and Prawn Parcels, p.46.

---

1 lb (500 g) medium couscous

sea salt and freshly ground black pepper

4 tablespoons olive oil

¼ lb (125 g) okra

¼ lb (125 g) French beans

¼ lb (125 g) frozen garden peas

● Place the couscous in a saucepan, adding about the same volume of water. Season with salt and pepper. Heat and simmer, covered, until all the liquid is absorbed (the couscous, when tested, should be soft on the outside with a bite in the centre). Stir in the olive oil.
● While the couscous is simmering, pare off the okra stalks without cutting into the pods. Wash and pat dry. Wash, top and tail the French beans. Steam both vegetables for 5 minutes, then rinse under cold running water (this is to preserve the bright emerald colour). Chop the vegetables finely, and add to the cooked couscous. Then add the defrosted peas. Adjust seasoning if necessary.
● Press the mixture into six individual moulds or one large mould. Leave for at least 15 minutes. Invert onto a serving dish or, for individual moulds, plates and serve.

Serves 6

Variation: One courgette and a few mange-touts, or one green pepper and one or two broccoli spears.

Scrambled Eggs with Tomatoes

The tomatoes are filled with scrambled eggs. I find that the cream gives the eggs the right texture. If you can, use the pretty purple chive flowers instead of the stems. Try this with Baked Cod with Sun-Dried Tomato Sauce, p.44, or Smoked Duck and Prunes, p.54.

---

6 tomatoes, medium-size

1 oz (25 g) butter

4 eggs

1 tablespoon fresh oregano leaves

salt and freshly ground black pepper

1 tablespoon cream

a few chive stems or flowers

● Cut off and reserve a 'hat' from each tomato and, using a small spoon, scoop out most of the flesh and all of the seeds. Place upside down on kitchen paper and let drain.
● In a heavy saucepan, melt the butter until it reaches the 'noisette' stage, when a nutty aroma escapes from the pan. Reduce the heat and immediately pour in the beaten eggs, oregano, salt and pepper. Stir constantly with a wooden spoon, until the eggs are evenly set, adding the cream at the last minute. Transfer immediately to a plate to stop the cooking process (which would continue in the hot saucepan so the eggs would be dry), and allow to cool.
● Just before serving, place the tomatoes on a serving dish and fill each one with some of the scrambled eggs. Scatter on top the finely chopped chive stems or the flowers with the petals plucked off. Replace the 'hats' and serve.

Serves 6

Top: *Couscous and Vegetable Mould, with Tomato and Parsley Sauce (p.20)*
Bottom: *Scrambled Eggs with Tomatoes*

Tomato and Ricotta Roulade

This rolled soufflé with a cheese filling looks pretty when cut in slices, showing three coloured spirals. It goes well with a mixed green salad, such as lamb's lettuce, curly endive and purslane (or sweet yellow rocket if available), lightly seasoned with walnut oil and lemon juice, and Squash and Radish Salad, p.74. I also serve it with Lentils with Yoghurt and Raw Spinach Sauce, p.28.

---

3 oz (85 g) butter

2 oz (60 g) plain flour

¼ pt/5 fl oz (150 ml) single cream, hot

2 eggs, separated

1 × 5 oz (140 g) tin concentrated tomato paste

nutmeg

salt and freshly ground pepper

½ lb (250 g) ricotta cheese

1 tablespoon sour cream

1 handful chopped flat-leaved parsley

• Preheat the oven to 375°F/190°C/Gas 5. Line a 15 × 12 in (40 × 30 cm) baking tray with greaseproof paper and butter it generously.
• Make a white sauce with the butter, flour and single cream. When cooked remove from the heat, stir in the egg yolks and tomato paste and season with nutmeg, salt and pepper. Whisk the egg whites until firm, but not stiff, and fold into the sauce. Spread the mixture evenly over the baking tray and bake for 25 minutes.
• Meanwhile, prepare the filling. In a bowl, mash the ricotta cheese with a fork, bind with sour cream and stir in the parsley. Season with salt and pepper. Set aside.
• Lay a damp cloth on a flat surface and turn out the roulade. Carefully peel off the greaseproof paper and neatly trim the edges of the baked mixture. Spread the filling lengthways down the centre and fold first one side, then the other over the middle, so that the roll remains the same length as the original roulade but only a third of the width. Place a large oiled piece of foil on top and turn the roll upside down. Slide a baking tray underneath – it will be easier to carry like this – and remove the cloth. Wrap the roulade tightly in the foil and chill it for at least 6 hours so that it holds its shape.
• Just before serving, unwrap the roulade and transfer it to an oblong serving dish.

Serves 6

Tomato and Parsley Sauce

This is a good accompaniment to the Couscous and Vegetable Mould, p.18, or the Watercress Mousse with Avocado, p.96. You can replace the parsley with fresh coriander.

---

2 very large tomatoes

¼ pt/5 fl oz (150 ml) sour cream or Greek yoghurt

1–2 dashes Worcester sauce

1 teaspoon soya sauce

salt and freshly ground black pepper

2 heaped tablespoons chopped flat-leaved parsley

• Place the tomatoes in a bowl and pour over some boiling water; leave for 1 minute. Drain the tomatoes and peel them, discarding the green calyx. Chop roughly and whizz in a food processor until they are reduced to a smooth purée. Add the sour cream (or yoghurt), Worcester sauce, soya sauce and seasoning, taking into account the saltiness of the two sauces. Stir in the flat-leaved parsley and transfer to a sauce boat or a pretty bowl for serving.

Makes about ¾ pt (½ litre)

Right: *Tomato and Ricotta Roulade*

Seaweed Omelette

For this recipe I usually use nori, a Japanese seaweed related to laverbread, which is sold dried in black sheets (and, incidentally, is used for wrapping sushi). The nori is gently cooked so that it becomes crispy and a green iridescent colour, which makes an attractive contrast with the omelette's deep yellow. This dish is delicious with Courgette and Leek Salad with Sage, p.79, and Saffron Bread, p.17, lightly toasted.

---

6 sheets nori

1 oz (25 g) butter

8 large eggs

½ tablespoon cream

sea salt and freshly ground black pepper

● Grill the sheets of seaweed at a low heat and toast lightly, turning once. Heat the butter in an omelette pan. Beat the eggs with the cream and season with salt and pepper. Make an omelette in the usual way; when almost set, crumble four seaweed sheets in an even layer, across one half of the omelette.
● Fold it over and turn onto a serving dish. Let cool. Just before serving, cut the omelette across in broad slices and crumble the remaining seaweed in between each cut.

Serves 4

Wholemeal Fusilli with Dill

I find that wholemeal pasta has a distinct, rather nutty flavour which here is combined with fresh-tasting peas and dill. You may replace the spiral-shaped fusilli with shell-like conchiglie. This dish makes a nice follow-up to Mussel and Courgette Soup, p.42, and is excellent with a tomato and fresh thyme salad and Turkey Rolls filled with bacon and broccoli purée, p.60.

---

1 lb (500 g) fresh wholemeal fusilli

3 tablespoons sesame oil

¼ pt/5 fl oz (150 ml) sour cream

1 bunch fresh dill

salt and freshly ground black pepper

8 oz (250 g) peas, shelled

● Fill a large saucepan with salted water and a teaspoon of oil and bring to a boil. Meanwhile, in a small bowl combine the sesame oil and sour cream, beating thoroughly. Add the chopped dill and season. Reserve.
● Pour some boiling water over the peas and leave for 3–4 minutes. Drain. Next, cook the fresh fusilli in the large saucepan for exactly 1 minute (or for 10–12 minutes if dried fusilli are used) and drain. Transfer to a serving bowl. Add the sauce, then toss in the peas until evenly distributed. Serve cold.

Serves 6–8

Top: *Seaweed Omelette*
Bottom: *Wholemeal Fusilli with Dill*

Spinach Fusilli with Cucumber and Yoghurt

The yoghurt sauce in this recipe is flavoured with soya sauce. The spiral-shaped fusilli hold a good quantity of fresh-tasting sauce. They are well complemented by Salt Cod with Coriander, p.42, or Smoked Trout Balls, p.50, and a pink grapefruit and watercress salad.

---

1 lb (500 g) spinach fusilli

½ cucumber, peeled and finely chopped

½ garlic clove, shaved

8 fl oz (250 ml) Greek yoghurt

2 teaspoons soya sauce

2 oz (60 g) slivered almonds, lightly toasted

salt and freshly ground black pepper

● Fill half a saucepan with salted water and bring to a fast boil. Cook the pasta for 10 to 12 minutes or until cooked al dente. Drain very thoroughly in a colander.
● In a bowl, blend together the cucumber, yoghurt, garlic shavings, soya sauce and almonds. Season and toss in the pasta.
● Serve at room temperature or chilled.

Serves 6

Buckwheat Kasha with Peas

Whole, husked buckwheat is called kasha in Russian cookery where it is used extensively. It can be compared with rice but has a more definite flavour. I buy kasha from health food shops. Serve with either Lettuce Purée or Shredded Radicchio, p.82 or Brussels Sprouts and Raisins with Paprika Mayonnaise, p.71. Kasha is also excellent with game and with Monkfish and Cucumber, p.53.

---

1 lb (500 g) kasha

3 fresh thyme sprigs

½ lb (250 g) frozen peas

3 tablespoons hazelnut oil

salt and freshly ground black pepper

● Place the kasha with twice its measure of water and the thyme in a saucepan and bring to a fast boil for 1 minute. Reduce the heat and simmer for 10 to 12 minutes or until it is cooked and all the liquid has evaporated.
● Stir in the frozen peas and hazelnut oil. Leave to cool. This will be enough time for the peas to be properly done. Season to taste and serve at room temperature.

Serves 6

Top: *Spinach Fusilli with Cucumber and Yoghurt* Bottom: *Buckwheat Kasha with Peas*

Hodsoll Salad

This salad was improvised with a friend one evening, using watercress left over in the refrigerator. It is a quickly made treat to serve with hot toast and a good bottle of chilled white wine. Serve with New Potato and Fennel Salad, p.69, or Smoked Duck and Prunes, p.54, or with a raw spinach salad.

---

2 bunches watercress

3 tablespoons mayonnaise

12 oz (340 g) cottage cheese

4 oz (125 g) Emmenthal cheese, coarsely grated

salt and freshly ground black pepper

4 soft-boiled eggs

a handful of flat-leaved parsley

finely grated nutmeg

● Cut off the ends of the watercress stems and discard any blemished or yellowed leaves. Chop finely by hand or in a food processor. Stir in the mayonnaise, cottage cheese and grated Emmenthal. Season. Then spread the mixture in a small gratin dish and place the shelled soft-boiled eggs on top. Scatter the parsley over the top of this, season with a few shavings of nutmeg, and serve.

Serves 2 to 4

Farfalle with Broccoli and Pine Nuts

The addition of pine nuts and raisins gives this pasta dish a rather exotic flavour. You may replace the butterfly-shaped farfalle with shell-like conchiglie. Try it with Chicken in Lemon and Tomato Aspic, p.62, or Mozzarella and Ricotta Salad with Anchovies, p.11.

---

1 lb (500 g) young broccoli, trimmed

1 lb (500 g) farfalle

2 oz (60 g) raisins

2 oz (60 g) pine nuts, lightly toasted

1 tablespoon fruity olive oil

salt and freshly ground black pepper

● Bring to the boil a large pan three-quarters filled with salted water. Boil the broccoli for 4 to 5 minutes, then remove from the water with a slotted spoon. Cool under cold running water. Chop the stems finely, keeping the florets intact, and set aside.
● Now cook the farfalle in the same boiling water used for the broccoli, for about 10 minutes or until they are soft outside but still crunchy in the centre. Drain and place in a bowl with the raisins, pine nuts and olive oil, tossing well. Season. When cooled, add the broccoli and serve.

Serves 6

Top: *Hodsoll Salad*
Bottom: *Farfalle with Broccoli and Pine Nuts*

Lentils with Yoghurt and Raw Spinach Sauce

For this dish try to get small green or brown lentils which have more flavour and do not disintegrate into a mush when cooked. Lentils, contrary to most pulses, do not need soaking. I buy fresh lemon grass root from an Asian delicatessen. You could serve this with Tomato and Ricotta Roulade, p.20, or Okra, Bacon and Ginger Salad, p.77. It is also delicious with Plaice with Walnut and Paprika Sauce, p.49, or Turkey Rolls, p.60.

---

1 lb (500 g) green or brown lentils

1 root fresh lemon grass

salt and freshly ground black pepper

½ lb (250 g) spinach

8 fl oz (250 ml) yoghurt

juice of 1 lemon

● Wash the lentils carefully, picking over in a colander to remove little stones or discoloured seeds. Place them and the outer leaves of the lemon grass root (reserving the centre) in a saucepan and cover generously with cold water and a little water to spare and bring very slowly to the boil. Simmer for 40 to 50 minutes or until soft but not mushy. Add some salt only towards the end of the cooking. Drain (reserving the liquid for a soup). Discard the lemon grass.
● Wash the spinach thoroughly several times, trimming off any long stems, then dry. Shred it finely and place in a bowl. Slice the remaining lemon grass and add to the spinach. Pour the yoghurt and lemon juice, beaten together, over this, season and toss. Add the spinach sauce to the lentils. Serve at room temperature.

Serves 6

From left to right: *Leek Shortcake (p.30), Lentils with Yoghurt and Raw Spinach Sauce, Green Ravioli with Pecorino Cheese and Basil (p.30)*

Green Ravioli with Pecorino Cheese and Basil

For this recipe I buy spinach ravioli stuffed with ricotta and spinach, but you could use green tortellini. If you like, serve this dish on a bed of thinly sliced tomatoes. It goes well with fish, poultry or veal, or, for a lighter meal, you could serve it with Shredded Radicchio, p.82. If pecorino cheese is not available use mature Cheddar or Double Gloucester instead.

1 lb (500 g) ravioli

½ lb (250 g) pecorino cheese, grated

6 fresh basil sprigs

6 tablespoons fruity olive oil

salt and coarsely ground black peppercorns

- Cook the pasta for 10–12 minutes in a large pan three-quarters filled with salted water.
- Meanwhile, in a soup plate mash, with a large fork, the cheese, torn basil leaves and olive oil until you obtain a thickish paste. Season and set on one side.
- When the ravioli are ready, drain and allow to cool for a few minutes.
- Transfer to a serving dish or shallow bowl and toss in the sauce. Eat without delay.

Serves 4 to 6

Leek Shortcake

The wholemeal flour gives a rather nutty flavour to the shortcake and goes well with the leeks and nutmeg. It is nice with Yellow Peppers with Spinach, p.91, or Beetroot and Celery Salad with Pistachios, p.73, or Egg Cups with Paprika, p.31. This, in fact, is one of those dishes which tastes delicious with many things.

6 oz (175 g) wholemeal flour

1½ teaspoons baking powder

salt

6 oz (175 g) butter

¼pt/5 fl oz (150 ml) buttermilk

1½ lb (750 g) leeks

2 eggs

7 fl oz (200 ml) single cream

nutmeg

- Preheat the oven to 425°F/220°C/Gas 7. Sift together the flour, baking powder and a pinch of salt. Cut 2 oz (60 g) of the butter in small pieces and rub it into the flour. Bind with enough buttermilk to make a firm dough. Turn onto a floured board. Knead once or twice. Reserve.
- Peel, slice and clean the leeks thoroughly. Melt the remaining butter in a heavy sauté pan, add the leeks and cook them gently until they are softened and a little transparent. Stir now and then to make sure they do not stick. In a small bowl beat the eggs and cream together and season with salt and nutmeg. Drain the leeks and add them to the egg and cream mixture. Check the seasoning, adding more salt and nutmeg if necessary.
- Sprinkle the work surface with flour and roll out the shortcake dough or flatten it with the floured heel of the hand until it is ¼ in (5 mm) thick. Put it into a 6 × 10 in (15 × 25 cm) rectangular shallow tin. Pour over the leek mixture and smooth it with the back of a spoon. Cook in the preheated oven for 25 minutes. Serve at room temperature, cut in broad slices.

Serves 6 to 8

Egg Cups with Paprika

The cups in this recipe are in fact the eggs' shells cut in half and filled. They look very attractive when brought to the table. Try serving them with Marinated Prawns and Cod with Thai Sauce, p.42, or Ham and Water Chestnut Parcels, p.59, or Mushrooms with Aubergines, p.92. They also go well with Melba toast and a green salad or with Leek Shortcake, p.30.

---

8 hard-boiled eggs

4 oz (125 g) butter

½ teaspoon paprika

1 tablespoon of finely chopped chives

salt and freshly ground black pepper

● With a very sharp kitchen knife halve the eggs lengthwise, shell and all. Don't worry if little bits of the shell break on the edges and become uneven; in the end it won't show.
● Scoop out the eggs carefully into a bowl and chop finely, using two knives to make this task easier. Trim the edges of the half shells and reserve. Melt the butter with most of the paprika, pour over the eggs and mix in with a large fork or potato masher. Add the chives and season to taste. With a small spoon, refill the half shells, pressing lightly but firmly, leaving the egg mixture slightly heaped. Leave to cool – the butter will set the mixture. Sprinkle with the remaining paprika and serve.

Serves 6–8

Chinese Noodles, Cheese and Coriander

In this recipe it is best to use a very light, nearly tasteless, grape-seed oil which coats the ingredients without detracting from the careful blend of flavours. This is delicious preceded by Mussel and Courgette Soup, p.42, and served with Smoked Trout Balls, p.50, or Smoked Duck and Prunes, p.54.

---

6 oz (175 g) Chinese egg noodles

3–4 tablespoons grape-seed oil

4 oz (125 g) Emmenthal, cut in julienne strips

4 oz (125 g) cashew nuts, lightly toasted

1 spring onion, cut into julienne strips

1 teaspoon black mustard seeds (optional)

sea salt and freshly ground black pepper

1 handful fresh coriander leaves

● Immerse the noodles in a saucepan filled with boiling water (in which you have placed the discarded coriander stems, so that the water is flavoured with them). Remove at once from the heat and leave for 6 minutes precisely. Drain. Transfer to a bowl and toss in the oil until the noodles are well coated. Let cool. Then add the Emmenthal, cashew nuts, split in two, the spring onion, and mustard seeds if you are using them. Season. Stir in the whole coriander leaves just before serving (any earlier and they would wilt and loose their delicate appearance).

Serves 4–6

Conchiglie with Ricotta and Basil Filling

The conchiglie used here are a giant shell-shaped pasta whose cavities are filled with white cheese and herbs (available from any good Italian grocer). They look very attractive and would go well with a tomato salad or the Beetroot and Celery Salad with Pistachios, p.73, followed by Pear Sorbet with Poached Pears, p.108.

14 oz (375 g) packet giant conchiglie

3 tablespoons olive oil

1½ lb (750 g) ricotta cheese

3 tablespoons sour cream

1 large bunch fresh basil (about 25 leaves)

salt and freshly ground black pepper

● Cook the giant conchiglie for 10–12 minutes in a large pan filled with salted boiling water. Drain. Toss the pasta and olive oil in a bowl until the conchiglie are coated and shiny. Season and allow to cool. Meanwhile, prepare the filling. Mash the ricotta and sour cream together in a bowl. Add most of the basil leaves, reserving about thirty.
● Fill each shell with a heaped teaspoon of the filling and insert a basil leaf on top.
● Serve from a flat serving dish.

Serves 6

From left to right: *Conchiglie with Ricotta and Basil Filling, Chinese Noodles, Cheese and Coriander (p.31), Egg Cups with Paprika (p.31)*

Savoury Cheese Mille-Feuille

I serve this mille-feuille as a starter, with seed-less grapes, divided into sprays, floating in a pretty glass bowl half-filled with water and ice, which creates a magnifying effect. The Brie may be replaced with other cheeses.

---

8 oz (250 g) puff pastry

2 oz (60 g) hazelnuts

6 oz (175 g) Brie cheese

2 oz (60 g) butter

1 tablespoon (15 ml) cognac (optional)

2 tablespoons Greek yoghurt

salt and freshly ground black pepper

1–2 sprigs fresh tarragon

- Preheat the oven to 450°F/230°C/Gas 8.
- Roll out the pastry into a rectangle about 12 × 6 in (30 × 15 cm). Place it on a baking sheet and bake for 25 minutes or until golden. Leave to cool. Switch off the oven and toast the hazelnuts for 5 to 7 minutes in it while there is still a strong heat. Let them cool for a few minutes, then, with heat-proof gloves on, rub off the skins, blowing off any remaining flakes over the sink. Chop coarsely, keeping some whole nuts aside for decoration.
- In a food processor, reduce the Brie and butter to a thick paste, and add the cognac if used. Add the yoghurt and blend lightly until all the ingredients are combined. Season well. Add the tarragon leaves, finely chopped.
- The pastry should be cooled by now, so, using a long knife, cut into three rectangles about 4 in (10 cm) wide. Then carefully separate each piece horizontally in two. Spread two-thirds of the cheese mixture equally over the bottom layers, covering them evenly, right to the edges. Scatter the chopped hazelnuts on top. Gently add the top layers of pastry and repeat the operation with the remaining ingredients, using the whole hazelnuts this time. To serve, cut each piece into two portions.

Serves 6

Tagliatelle and Crayfish

The crayfish are served on a bed of tagliatelle laced with a creamy sauce so that each person shells his or her own crayfish and places the debris on a side plate. Place several finger bowls on the table. Serve with a lettuce heart and watercress salad or perhaps the Broccoli, Avocado and Red Pepper Salad, p.73. The Skordalia Ramequins, right, would be a good appetizer.

---

1 lb (500 g) tagliatelle

½ pt/10 fl oz (300 ml) double cream

1 tablespoon cognac

salt and freshly ground black pepper

zest of ½ orange, finely grated

2 oz (60 g) pine nuts, lightly toasted

2 lb (1 kg) cooked crayfish

- Bring a large pan three-quarters filled with salted water to the boil. Cook the pasta for 10 to 12 minutes.
- Meanwhile beat together the cream and cognac and season with salt and pepper. Stir in the orange zest and the pine nuts.
- Drain the pasta and, in a bowl, toss in the creamy sauce. Allow to cool.
- Serve at room temperature with the crayfish arranged on top.

Serves 4 to 6

Skordalia Ramequins

This is an adaption from a Greek sauce that is usually eaten with salted fish. The name derives from 'skortho', Greek for garlic. Serve with Melba toast as a starter, or, as a main course, with Tagliatelle and Crayfish (left), and Belgian endives, leaves separated and presented petal-like on a small plate. These ramequins also make a nice accompaniment for Sole Fillets Primavera, p.39.

---

4 garlic cloves

a few grains coarse sea salt

4 oz (125 g) pine nuts or almonds, freshly ground

4 slices white bread

½ pt (300 ml) olive oil

juice of 2 lemons

Greek yoghurt

- Peel the garlic and chop it finely (removing the green shoot embedded in the centre if necessary). Pound it in a mortar, with the sea salt, to a smooth mush. Add the ground pine nuts or almonds, then the bread, which has been soaked 5 minutes in water and squeezed dry. Pour in the oil, drop by drop, exactly as you would for a mayonnaise. Lastly add the lemon juice and enough Greek yoghurt to obtain a firm but supple mixture. Transfer into eight ramequins and smooth evenly on top before serving.
- Serve immediately or chill.

Makes 8 ramequins

Left: *Tagliatelle and Crayfish*
Right: *Skordalia Ramequins*

Sole Fillets Primavera

In this recipe the fish is steamed between two plates on a bed of rosemary which imparts its aroma to the fillets. For an extra herbal flavour fresh basil leaves may be added after cooking as a garnish. Try this with Green Ravioli with Pecorino Cheese and Basil, p.30, or Skordalia Ramequins, p.36. For a lighter meal, simply accompany with a watercress and cottage cheese salad.

3–4 rosemary sprigs

4 lemon sole fillets

½ lb (250 g) peas, shelled

1 broccoli spear

sea salt and freshly ground black pepper

a little fruity olive oil

3–4 fresh basil leaves (optional)

● Use a pan and two soup plates which will sit neatly on the rim of the pan to steam the fish. Fill the pan halfway with water and bring to the boil. Place the rosemary sprigs on one plate and lay the fillets on top. Slice the broccoli once lengthwise and place on one side of the fish, piling the peas on the other. Season. Cover this with the other plate, upside down, and place both over the gently simmering water. Cook for 6 minutes. Wearing heatproof gloves, remove the top plate and leave the fish to cool. Dribble a little olive oil and the torn basil leaves, if desired, on top.

Serves 2

Croissant with Smoked Cod

For this recipe I buy a giant croissant which I then fill with yellow creamy cod. It looks quite spectacular when brought to the table. You may replace the giant croissant with four to six normal ones. You might serve this with Watercress Mousse with Avocado, p.96, or with Broccoli, Avocado and Red Pepper Salad, p.73.

---

1 lb (500 g) smoked cod

a few saffron stigmas

juice of ½ lemon

3 tablespoons olive oil

¼ pt (150 ml) single cream

freshly ground black pepper

● Remove the skin and bones from the smoked cod and cut into medium-sized pieces. Crush the saffron with a mortar, making sure you reserve every particle. Place the fish and saffron in a food processor. Reduce to a paste, then switch off the food processor and add the lemon juice. Re-run the motor and, in a stream through a funnel, pour in the olive oil. Lastly stir in the cream and season with plenty of freshly ground black pepper.
● With a long serrated knife cut the croissant in two horizontally and scoop out a little of the doughy centre. Pour in the smoked fish mixture and serve.

Serves 4

Top: *Sole Fillets Primavera*
Bottom: *Croissant with Smoked Cod*

Marinated Scallops and Fried Seaweed

The 'seaweed' used in this recipe is in fact shredded spring greens (which, incidentally, can be replaced with cabbage). The carambola, or star fruit, is a tropical fruit native to Indonesia, with a delicate translucent greenish-yellow colour and a characteristic star shape when sliced. It has a pleasant sweetish-sourness which goes well with scallops. Serve with Coral Sauce (right). Accompany with Petits-Pois Mould, p.77, Asparagus and Carrot Salad with Pine Nuts, p.83, or the Avocado, Cranberry and Orange Salad, p.88, or simply with Saffron Bread, p.17.

12 scallops

juice of 3 limes

1 tablespoon olive oil

salt and freshly ground black pepper

1 tablespoon Pernod (optional)

1 carambola (or star) fruit

½ lb (250 g) spring greens

oil for deep frying

● First chill the white parts of the scallops (reserving the coral) to make them firmer. Then with a sharp knife cut each one horizontally into three or four slices. Place in a dish and pour over the lime juice and olive oil, beaten together and seasoned. Let marinate for between 1 hour and 3 hours. Drain.
● Slice the carambola very thinly across. Alternate the carambola with the scallop slices on a serving dish in a circular design. Sprinkle over the Pernod if desired.
● Shred the spring greens finely and deep-fry in batches for about 1 minute. Drain and season. When all the 'seaweed' is done, pile in the centre of the dish and serve.

Serves 4–6

Coral Sauce

Perfect with Marinated Scallops and Fried Seaweed (left), this sauce can also be served with eggs or steamed vegetable dishes, such as broccoli or new potatoes. You can also omit the cream and use the coral mixture as a spread for small croûtons.

12 small scallop corals

4–5 tablespoons olive oil

about 1 tablespoon cream

salt and freshly ground black pepper

● Place the corals in a food processor and reduce to a purée. Then, with the motor still running, pour in the oil in a stream. Thin to the consistency of a mayonnaise, stirring in the cream. Season to taste and serve.

Makes about ½ pt (300 ml)

Clockwise from left: *Marinated Scallops and Fried Seaweed with Coral Sauce, Tuna and French Bean Salad (p.43), Mussel and Courgette Soup (p.42)*

Mussel and Courgette Soup

This soup is particularly good with grated cheese or sour cream. Serve with Saffron Bread, p.17, and follow it, perhaps, with Seaweed Omelette, p.22.

---

4 pt (2 litres) mussels

1 oz (25 g) butter

6 fl oz (180 ml) white wine

2 lb (1 kg) courgettes

1 large leek, white only

2 garlic cloves

1–2 saffron threads

sea salt and freshly ground black pepper

● Discard any open or broken mussels and scrub the remainder in cold water using a small brush. Pull away any beards and, using a sharp knife, scrape off any barnacles.
● Place the mussels in a large pan with half the butter, the white wine and plenty of pepper. Cover and cook for 5 minutes, shaking the pan once or twice. All the shells should be open by now, so discard any which have remained closed. Remove the flesh and reserve it. Filter the mussels' liquid through a fine sieve or muslin and reserve.
● Chop the cleaned leek; wipe and finely slice the courgettes. In a clean saucepan, heat the remaining butter. Add the courgettes and the leek and sauté for 5 minutes. Then add the finely crushed garlic, saffron and mussels' liquid, adding to it about 6 fl oz (180 ml) of hot water. Season. Cook, uncovered, for 15 minutes, adding the mussels at the last minute. Check the seasoning and adjust accordingly. Serve at room temperature or chilled.

Serves 6

Salt Cod with Coriander

Here the cod is cooked to a creamy mass which is piled on a bed of spinach. The fragrant coriander goes well with the rather bland cod. Serve with a tomato and broccoli salad or a Belgian endive, walnut and apple salad. Spinach Fusilli with Cucumber and Yoghurt, p.25, is another delicious accompaniment.

1½ lb (750 g) salt cod

4 tablespoons olive oil

8 fl oz (250 ml) sour cream

1 handful fresh coriander

1 lb (500 g) spinach

● Soak the salt cod for 24 hours, changing the cold water two or three times. After the last rinse, pat dry and slice in thin strips, discarding the skin and any bones.
● Heat the olive oil in a frying pan and, when hot, add the cod and stir constantly with a wooden spoon. The mixture will become a white mass as the fish disintegrates into it.
● Beat together the sour cream and coriander and pour quickly over the cod. Remove from the heat and let cool.
● Meanwhile, scrupulously wash the spinach several times until thoroughly clean. Trim off most of the stem, then, with a sharp knife, shred finely. On a serving dish make a 'nest' with the spinach. Spoon the cod mixture into the centre.

Serves 6

Marinated Prawns and Cod with Thai Sauce

This makes a colourful dish with the yellow iridescent cod and the pinkish hue of the prawns, both wrapped in emerald green mange-touts. Try this after Celeriac and Fresh

Coriander Soup, p.67, and accompany with something like the Lettuce Purée, p.82, or Egg Cups with Paprika, p.31.

---

2 lb (1 kg) prawns

1½ lb (750 g) smoked cod

3 tablespoons cognac or dry sherry

salt and freshly ground black pepper

½ lb (250 g) mange-touts

————————— *Thai Sauce* —————————

½ packet (4 oz/125 g) creamed coconut

½ pt (300 ml) hot water

12 oz (340 g) cashew nuts, freshly ground

1 tablespoon brown sugar

a little cayenne pepper

1 tablespoon soya sauce

salt and freshly ground black pepper

● Peel and devein the prawns, leaving the tails on. Cut the cod in long thin strips about ½ in (2 cm) wide. Place the prawns and cod in a bowl, add the cognac or dry sherry and season. Let marinate for at least an hour, then drain and reserve the liquid.
● String the mange-touts and steam for 30 seconds, then immerse in a bowl filled with iced water. Drain and set aside.
● For the sauce, melt the creamed coconut with the hot water in a heavy saucepan, stirring constantly. Add the ground cashew nuts, sugar, cayenne pepper, soya sauce and the marinade from the prawns and cod. Taste and adjust the seasoning accordingly. Transfer to a bowl and cover until needed. Let cool but do not refrigerate.
● Wrap separately each prawn and smoked cod strip in a mange-tout and secure with a stick. Arrange on a dish and serve with the sauce on the side.

Serves 6 to 8

Tuna and French Bean Salad

The French green beans are cooked only until al dente and still crunchy. They contrast nicely with the tuna's texture and taste. Try serving with Potato, Turnip and Radicchio Salad, p.67, preceded by Tomato and Coconut Soup, p.66.

---

1 lb (500 g) small French beans

2 × 3–4 oz (100 g) tins of tuna fish chunks in oil

1 tablespoon olive oil

1 teaspoon fennel seeds

salt and freshly ground black pepper

● Top and tail the French beans and steam them for 2 to 3 minutes. Cool them swiftly under cold running water or immerse in a bowl filled with iced water. Drain.
● Flake the fish and toss with the olive oil, French beans and fennel seeds. Season to your taste and serve.

Serves 4 to 6

Baked Cod with Sun-Dried Tomato Sauce

The rather bland taste of this fish is here enhanced with a rich sauce. Sun-dried tomato paste has a smoky flavour, and can be obtained from good delicatessens. As it is quite salty already, I omit salt altogether from this recipe. This dish goes well with steamed French beans and watercress and Citrons Confits, p. 80. Or try it with Scrambled Eggs with Tomatoes, p. 18.

---

a little olive oil

1½ lb (750 g) cod fillets

2–3 sprigs fresh oregano

6 oz (180 g) jar of sun-dried tomato paste

2 eggs, hard-boiled

8 fl oz (250 ml) sour cream

coarsely crushed black pepper

● Preheat the oven to 400°F/200°C/Gas 6. Lightly oil a piece of foil and place the cod on it. Place the oregano sprigs on top and fold into a neat parcel, making sure the edges are tightly closed. Place on a baking tray and bake for 15 minutes. Remove from the oven and let cool, still wrapped.
● Meanwhile, beat together the sun-dried tomato paste and the finely chopped hard-boiled eggs. Stir in the sour cream. The sauce should be rather thick.
● Spoon the sauce onto a serving dish. Carefully place the fish on top of the sauce, and scatter the pepper over the fish.

Serves 6

From left to right: *Salt Cod with Coriander (p. 42) Baked Cod with Sun-dried Tomato Sauce, Marinated Prawns and Cod with Thai Sauce*

Mussel and Prawn Parcels

Here individual cabbage leaves are wrapped around a shellfish filling so that they look like tiny whole cabbages. If you like you can buy prepared mussels sold in cartons. Serve with Lemon Sauce (right). Try serving also with Couscous and Vegetable Mould, p.18.

---

8 medium-sized Savoy cabbage leaves

2 lb (1 kg) mussels

2 pt (1.25 litres) cooked prawns, shelled and deveined

5 juniper berries, lightly crushed

about ½ lb (250 g) cooked rice

2 tablespoons sour cream

salt and freshly ground black pepper

● Steam the cabbage for 2 to 3 minutes and swiftly cool under cold running water, thereby preserving the green colour. Pat dry and reserve.
● Discard any broken mussels and scrub the rest with a small brush under cold running water. Pull away any beards and, using a sharp knife, scrape off any barnacles. Discard any mussels which remain open when lightly tapped. Place the mussels in a large pan, cover and leave over a high heat for about 5 minutes or until the shells are all open, shaking the pan once or twice.
● Drain the mussels over a bowl, reserving the liquid which can be used for a soup. Discard any shells which have remained closed. Remove the flesh from each mussel with a partly open empty shell (using it as you would tongs) and chop.
● In a bowl place the mussels, chopped prawns, juniper berries, rice and sour cream. Season. Lay a cabbage leaf flat and place some of the filling near the stem. If necessary, trim off the centre stem so that the leaves fold more easily. Fold sides over, then roll towards the leaf end, making a neat parcel. Repeat with the remaining ingredients.

Serves 4

Lemon Sauce

This sharp-tasting sauce, excellent with Mussel and Prawn Parcels (left), is also delicious with green vegetables. It is not necessary to use homemade mayonnaise.

---

2 slices of white bread, crust cut off

6 tablespoons milk

½ pt (300 ml) mayonnaise

juice of 2 lemons

salt and freshly ground black pepper

● Soak the bread in the milk and leave for a few minutes, then squeeze dry. Place the bread in a bowl and mash in with the mayonnaise, thinning it down with lemon juice. You should have a firm but supple sauce. Season to taste and serve.

Makes ¾ pt (½ litre)

Right: *Mussel and Prawn Parcels with Lemon Sauce*

Plaice with Walnut and Paprika Sauce

Here the fish's juices and cooked lemon slices are added to the sauce to make it very flavourful and sharp. It is excellent with Lentils with Yoghurt and Raw Spinach Sauce, p.28, Petits-Pois Mould, p.77, or Broad Beans and Baby Carrots with Savory, p.64, and Citrons Confits, p.80. For a simpler meal, just accompany with steamed new potatoes.

4 plaice, filleted

salt and freshly ground black pepper

½ tablespoon oil

½ lemon, thinly sliced

For Sauce

3 oz (90 g) walnuts, finely ground

1 teaspoon paprika

5 tablespoons walnut oil

● Preheat the oven to 350°F/180°C/Gas 4. Place the fish fillets, seasoned in two layers, on a large piece of oiled foil, with the lemon slices in the centre. Close the foil tightly, making a 'papillotte', and bake the plaice for 10 minutes. Remove from the oven and let cool in the parcel. Transfer the drained fish fillets to a serving dish. Reserve.
● Pour boiling water over the walnuts and leave for a few minutes. Remove the lemon slices (discarding any pips) and place them along with the juices gathered in the foil in a food processor. Blend until reduced to a pulp. Turn off the food processor and add the walnuts, paprika and walnut oil. Process again until the ingredients form a homogeneous mixture, adding a little more oil if the sauce is too thick. Adjust seasoning, spoon over the fish and serve.

Serves 6

Left: *Smoked Salmon and Watercress Soup*
Right: *Plaice with Walnut and Paprika Sauce*

Smoked Salmon and Watercress Soup

This is quite a substantial soup, with the complementary flavours of salmon and watercress, which should be followed with a rather light course, such as Radicchio, Bean Shoot and Mint Salad, p.79.

8 oz (250 g) smoked salmon trimmings

3 bunches watercress

1½ pt (900 ml) chicken stock

½ pt/10 fl oz (300 ml) sour cream

juice of 1 lemon

freshly ground black pepper

● Reserve one nice piece of salmon for decoration. Roughly chop the remainder of the salmon trimmings, discarding bones and bits of skin if necessary. Reduce to a purée in a food processor and place in a bowl. Set aside.
● Discard any toughened watercress stems and any blemished or yellowed leaves. Chop the remainder finely and add to the salmon. Stir in the stock, sour cream and lemon juice. Season with pepper only, as the salmon will impart its saltiness to the other ingredients. Chill until needed. Decorate with the reserved salmon.

Serves 6

Rainbow Trout in Filo Pastry

In this recipe paper-thin layers of pastry conceal a tantalizing filling of rainbow trout and creamed watercress. The best way to deal with the filo pastry is to work with one sheet at a time, leaving the remainder covered with a damp cloth or a plastic bag to prevent them becoming brittle. This dish goes well with Avocado Ice, p.88, or Okra, Bacon and Ginger Salad, p.77.

3 bunches watercress

½ pt 10 fl oz (300 ml) sour cream

3 hard-boiled eggs, chopped

juice of 1 lemon

salt and freshly ground black pepper

walnut oil

14 sheets filo pastry

3 rainbow trout, about 12 oz (340 g) each, skinned and filleted

• Preheat the oven to 400°F/200°C/Gas 6.
• Steam the watercress for 1 minute, then cool under cold running water. In a food processor or by hand, reduce to a purée and add the sour cream. Stir in the chopped eggs, lemon juice and season.
• You will need an ovenproof dish or tin about 8 in (20 cm) square and 1½ in (4 cm) deep. Brush the inside of the dish or tin lightly with walnut oil, then brush two sheets of filo pastry and press them down, on top of each other, to line the dish. The edges will overhang the dish, which is correct, as they will be used to fold over the finished dish. Brush five pastry sheets with oil and place them in the bottom.
• Spread half the watercress mixture over the pastry, place the fish fillets on top (removing any bones that you come across) and cover with the remaining watercress mixture. Season, lay a lightly oiled pastry sheet on top and continue adding the remaining sheets, oiling each layer. Now fold over the overhanging pieces of filo,

pushing in the corners for a neat fit. Oil the surface and bake for 25 to 30 minutes, or until golden on top. Let cool.
• To serve, cut diagonally into wedges.

Serves 6

Smoked Trout Balls

These spiky green balls look rather attractive presented on a bed of shredded radicchio or simply on a wicker tray with a selection of rye biscuits. This light dish can be served with Spinach Fusilli with Cucumber and Yoghurt, p.25, or Chinese Noodles, Cheese and Coriander, p.31.

2 smoked trout

3 oz (85 g) strong hot horseradish sauce

4 oz (125 g) cream cheese, at room temperature

juice of ½ lemon

1 teaspoon of black mustard seeds (optional)

1 bunch of flat-leaved parsley, finely chopped

• Remove the skin and flesh from the smoked trout, discarding any bones. Place the flesh in a bowl and mash it with the horseradish, then add the cream cheese, lemon juice and mustard seeds, if desired. Refrigerate the mixture until it is firm enough to work with your hands, and roll into about twelve balls. Then roll each ball on the parsley to create a spiky green effect.

Makes about 12 portions

Left: *Rainbow Trout in Filo Pastry*
Right: *Smoked Trout Balls*

Monkfish and Cucumber

In this recipe the fish is wrapped with cucumber ribbons in a spiral fashion. The cucumber is used both for the fish recipe, and for the sauce – steamed for the former, raw for the latter. Serve with Cucumber and Dill Sauce (right). This goes well with Buckwheat Kasha with Peas, p.25, and Avocado Ice, p.88.

1½ lb (750 g) boned monkfish

1 tablespoon melted butter

salt and freshly ground black pepper

1 cucumber

● Cut the monkfish crosswise into eight to ten slices, brushing them with butter and seasoning each one. Cut the cucumber in half. Peel one half with a vegetable peeler and then cut lengthways into eight to ten long thin slices, reserving the other half for the sauce. Wrap each piece of fish with a cucumber ribbon in a spiral fashion. Place, with seam down, in a steamer and steam for 5 minutes. Leave to cool and serve with the sauce in a separate dish.

Serves 4

Left: *Monkfish and Cucumber with Cucumber and Dill Sauce*

Cucumber and Dill Sauce

The perfect accompaniment to Monkfish and Cucumber, left, this sauce is also delicious served with small new potatoes. You will need about half a cucumber, which should be left from the previous recipe. For a richer sauce replace some of the yoghurt with mayonnaise.

½ cucumber

½ pt/10 fl oz (300 ml) yoghurt

1 tablespoon chopped fresh dill

salt and pepper

● In a food processor or by hand, finely chop the cucumber. Add the yoghurt and stir in the dill. Season. Serve chilled.

Makes about ¾ pt (⅓ litre)

Steamed Chicken Balls

I buy most of the ingredients for this dish from Chinese grocers. The chicken balls may be prepared ahead of time and steamed later. I serve them straight from the bamboo basket in which they are steamed, with a pile of lettuce leaves on the side so that the balls can be wrapped in a leaf and eaten with the fingers. Try them with Sorrel and Mustard Sauce, p.56, and Rice and Parmesan Salad, p.11.

---

5 oz (150 g) glutinous rice

4–5 scented dried Chinese mushrooms

1 lb (500 g) boned smoked chicken

1 egg, lightly beaten

2 teaspoons soya sauce

1 in (2.5 cm) piece fresh ginger root, finely chopped

1 × 8 oz (250 g) tin water chestnuts, chopped

a little fresh coriander, finely chopped

lettuce leaves

● Place the rice in a bowl, cover with water and let it soak for 4 hours. Drain and pat dry. Also soak the mushrooms in a little warm water for 1 hour, then drain them. Cut off the tough stems and discard. Chop the caps finely.
● In a food processor, reduce the chicken to a mince. In a bowl mix together the mushrooms, chicken, egg, soya sauce, ginger, water chestnuts and coriander (your hands are best for this task), until well combined. Form small balls of the mixture, each 1¼ in (3 cm) in diameter.
● Spread the rice on a baking sheet and roll the chicken balls in it, one at a time, coating them completely. Place the balls on waxed paper and refrigerate for at least 1 hour. (At this point the balls can be frozen.) Steam the balls, in one layer (I use two or three bamboo steaming baskets for this, depending on their size) for 15 minutes. Allow the chicken balls to cool.

Makes about 30 balls

Smoked Duck and Prunes

For this dish a thin slice of smoked duck is wrapped around a spiced prune and the roll is secured with a stick. Bamboo saté sticks look nicer than ordinary cocktail sticks. The former are available from Asian grocers. Try this with Fromage de Celeri, p.15, or Chinese Noodles, Cheese and Coriander, p.31.

---

12 giant prunes

China tea

1 piece of cinnamon bark

12 whole almonds

6 slices of smoked duck

● Soak the prunes in the strongly brewed tea with the cinnamon. Leave for 1–2 hours.
● Drain the prunes, slit them lengthwise and remove the stones, replacing each stone with a whole almond. Cut the smoked duck slices in two and wrap each half around a prune, securing on top with a wooden stick.
● Place on a wicker tray or flat dish to serve.

Serves 4

Left: *Smoked Duck and Prunes*
Right: *Steamed Chicken Balls*

Veal and Pistachio

The veal is braised with fennel then served cold with a piquant sorrel and mustard sauce (right). The sharpness of the sorrel contrasts beautifully with the blandness of the meat. When sliced the veal shows dots of green pistachio. Serve with Baby Corn and Broad Beans with Basil and Poppy Seeds, p.96, and Cherry Consommé, p.66, or try it with Green Ravioli with Pecorino Cheese and Basil, p.30.

2 lb (1 kg) boneless loin of veal, rolled and tied securely

about 20 pistachio nuts

1 oz (25 g) butter

1 fennel bulb, sliced lengthways

1 bay leaf

dry cider

salt and freshly ground black pepper

● Preheat the oven to 325°F/160°C/Gas 3.
● Make a few incisions in the veal and lard it with the pistachios. Melt the butter in a roasting pan and brown the meat all over. Remove the meat from the pan, add the fennel and sauté until it is a golden colour.
● Drain off all the fat, replace the fennel in the roasting pan and lay the meat on top. Season well. Add the bay leaf and pour over enough cider just to cover the bottom of the pan. Cover the pan with foil and braise in the oven for about 2 hours. Let the meat cool, still covered with the foil, out of the oven.
● Just before serving, drain off the meat and fennel juices. Thinly slice the veal and place, slightly overlapping, on a serving dish. Arrange the fennel in the centre. Serve the sauce separately.

Serves 6

Sorrel and Mustard Sauce

This sauce goes well with eggs, steamed fish, new potatoes and baby carrots, as well as the Veal and Pistachio, or Steamed Chicken Balls, p.54. Although quite different in flavour, you could replace sorrel, when it is not available, with watercress.

2 egg yolks, at room temperature

1 heaped teaspoon strong French mustard

salt

6–8 green peppercorns, lightly crushed

7 fl oz (200 ml) olive oil

2 bunches sorrel, chopped, with stems removed

juice of ½ lemon

about 2 tablespoons Greek yoghurt

● In a small bowl, beat together the egg yolks, mustard, salt and green peppercorns. Add the oil slowly, in a thin stream, beating constantly. Continue beating until all the oil has been incorporated and the sauce is emulsified and rather thick. Stir in the finely chopped sorrel. Thin down with the lemon juice and enough Greek yoghurt to obtain a slightly runny sauce.

Makes about 12 fl oz (350 ml)

Right: *Veal and Pistachio with Sorrel and Mustard Sauce*

Prosciutto and Watercress Spirals

In this recipe the watercress omelettes can be prepared as much as 12 hours ahead of time. They look pretty when sliced, spiral-like, showing layers of green and red. You could replace the prosciutto or Parma ham with coppa or smoked salmon. Try serving with Avocado Ice p.88, and Baby Corn and Broad Beans with Poppy Seeds, p.96.

——————— *For the filling:* ———————

4 oz (125 g) thinly sliced prosciutto

1 oz (25 g) cream or curd cheese

4 fl oz (125 ml) cream

1 teaspoon lemon juice

1 level tablespoon fresh dill, chopped

——————— *For the omelettes:* ———————

6 eggs

2 bunches watercress, trimmed and finely chopped

salt and freshly ground black pepper

1 tablespoon soda water or beer

butter

• By hand or in a food processor, finely chop the ham, then bind thoroughly with the cheese, cream, butter, lemon juice and dill. Set on one side.
• Beat the eggs thoroughly with the chopped watercress, salt and pepper, adding the soda water or beer last (either gives a light texture). In a 6 in (15 cm) lightly buttered omelette pan, make (in turn) six very thin omelettes, rather like pancakes, without turning them over. Pile onto a plate and cover. Continue until all the egg mixture is used. Allow to cool.

Left: *Ham and Water Chestnut Parcels*
Right: *Prosciutto and Watercress Spirals*

• Carefully lift one omelette and place it on a wooden board. Spread with some of the filling and roll. Place, seam down, on a large piece of greased foil. Repeat with each omelette and the rest of the filling. Wrap the rolls tightly and refrigerate for at least 1 hour, or until they are firm enough to slice.
• Just before serving unwrap and slice crossways, into spirals.

Makes 6 omelettes

Ham and Water Chestnut Parcels

These are bite-size appetizers. The water chestnuts' crunchiness goes well with the ham's texture. The parcels can also be eaten with a tossed green salad, coated with some of the dressing. They are also nice with Petit-Pois Mould, p.77, or Aubergine Flan with Coriander, p.92.

12 thin slices Parma ham

1 × 8 oz (250 g) tin water chestnuts, drained

freshly ground black pepper

3–4 fresh thyme sprigs, chopped

a little olive oil

• Cut the ham slices in two. Do the same with the water chestnuts and wrap them in the ham, seasoning the chestnuts first with pepper and thyme. With the tips of your fingers, pat the parcels with oil to keep them moist.

Makes about 24 parcels

Rabbit and Tongue Terrine

In this terrine the rather dry rabbit is well complemented by the tongue. When sliced, the terrine shows white, pink and green layers.

8 rabbit pieces

½ tablespoon oil

1 oz (25 g) butter

salt and freshly ground black pepper

about ½ pt (300 ml) light ale

½ pt (300 ml) chicken stock

1 sachet (about ½ oz/12 g) gelatine

1 bunch fresh tarragon

4 rather thick slices of pressed tongue

• Sauté the rabbit pieces in the mixture of oil and butter until golden. Season. Add the beer, cover and cook on a medium heat for about 25 minutes, adding more beer if necessary. Drain and bone the rabbit. Then cut the flesh across in medium-sized pieces. Strain the beer and juices into a muslin cloth or sieve and add the stock to them. Reheat this liquid and sprinkle with the gelatine, stirring until well dissolved. Allow to cool.
• Strip the tarragon leaves from their stems and cut each leaf roughly into two halves. Cube the tongue. Line the bottom and sides of a 2 pt (1 litre) terrine dish with a little cooled gelatine. I place the dish in the freezer beforehand so that the gelatine sets immediately.
• Place half the rabbit pieces in an even layer at the bottom of the terrine, then scatter over some tarragon. Add the tongue in one layer, followed by the remaining tarragon. Finish with the rest of the rabbit on top. Pour over the gelatine, evening the top gently with the back of a spoon.
• Leave to set for at least 12 hours in a refrigerator. Just before serving cut into thickish slices, taking care not to break them.

Serves 6

Turkey Rolls

For this dish the turkey escalopes are rolled up with bacon and broccoli purée. The latter may be replaced successfully with green beans or spinach. They are served sliced, so showing the pink and green layers. Try them with Lentils with Yoghurt and Raw Spinach Sauce, p.28, Rice and Parmeson Salad, p.11, or Wholemeal Fusilli with Dill, p.22.

4 oz (125 g) broccoli

4 turkey escalopes

3–4 sprigs fresh thyme

8 slices streaky bacon

salt and freshly ground black pepper

1 tablespoon oil

½ tablespoon butter

• Preheat the oven to 350°F/180°C/Gas 4. Trim the broccoli and steam for 6 minutes, cool under cold running water and purée in a food processor. Set aside.
• Flatten the escalopes with a meat cleaver (if you do not possess one ask your butcher to do so or, like me, use a heavy marble pastry roller). Pluck the thyme from the stems and scatter it over the turkey. If necessary, remove the rind from the bacon, then place two bacon slices on each escalope. Place a little of the broccoli purée in the centre. Roll each escalope and tie with a piece of string.
• In a frying pan heat the oil and butter and sauté the rolls for a few minutes (just enough to seal the juices). Transfer to an ovenproof dish and cook in the preheated oven for a further 20 minutes. Let cool and serve sliced.

Serves 6

Top: *Rabbit and Tongue Terrine*
Bottom: *Turkey Rolls*

Chicken in Lemon and Tomato Aspic

The aspic here sets without the addition of gelatine, but you may add ⅓ packet of gelatine if you want a firmer texture. Excellent with a lamb's lettuce and watercress salad.

---

2 bacon rashers

about 3 lb (1.5 kg) boiling fowl, dressed

10 cloves

1 celery heart

1–2 sprigs each fresh thyme and marjoram

about 3–4 pts (1.5–2 litres) water or chicken stock

salt and freshly ground black pepper

juice and grated rind of 1 lemon

5 oz (142 g) tin tomato paste

● Put the bacon at the bottom of a deep, heavy pan. With the tip of a blade, make some ten cuts in the fowl and insert the cloves. Chop the celery and place it in the bottom of the pan with the fowl on top. Add the thyme and marjoram and pour over the water or stock.
● Bring to a boil, skim and cover. Simmer for about 1 hour and 45 minutes or until the legs can be pulled easily and the flesh between them and the breast is barely pink. Remove the pan from the heat. Leave for 3 hours in a cool place.
● Remove the fowl from the stock and set aside. Strain and boil the stock down to about 1¾ pts (1 litre), then remove from the heat and degrease it by floating a piece of kitchen paper on top. Repeat the operation if necessary. Allow to cool and then stir in the lemon juice and rind and tomato paste. Disjoint the fowl; carve as many shapely pieces as you can from the breasts. Fit all the pieces snugly into an oblong straight-sided dish. Pour over the cooled stock and refrigerate until set – about 6 hours or overnight. Serve from the dish or unmould, in which case set the aspic with extra gelatine.

Serves 4–6

Chicken in Red Wine

In this recipe the chicken thighs are first marinated, then baked with oregano and finally honey-glazed under a grill. For the marinade I use a good leftover claret, if possible. Serve with brown rice with raisins and toasted nuts, and a green salad.

---

8 chicken thighs or drumsticks

½ pt (250 ml) red wine

sea salt and freshly ground black pepper

1 tablespoon olive oil

1 scant tablespoon dried (or 2 tablespoons fresh) oregano leaves

3 tablespoons clear honey

● In a shallow bowl, marinate the chicken pieces in the wine, seasoned with salt and pepper, for 12–48 hours.
● Preheat the oven to 400°F/200°C/Gas 6. Drain the chicken, discarding the marinade, and place on a large piece of foil. With the tips of your fingers, rub the thighs or drumsticks all over with the oil. Sprinkle with the oregano and season with salt and pepper. Wrap the chicken tightly in the foil, making a double seam, and place on a baking tray. Cook in the preheated oven for 25–30 minutes.
● Remove from the heat and allow to cool (still wrapped) for a few minutes. Open the parcel and brush the top of the chicken pieces with honey. Grill until they look crisp and shiny. Allow to cool and serve at room temperature.

Serves 4–6

Top: *Chicken in Lemon and Tomato Aspic*
Bottom: *Chicken in Red Wine*

Broad Beans and Baby Carrots with Savory

It would be ideal to have a kitchen garden for the ingredients here, as it would allow you to pick the youngest broad beans and tiniest carrots. Serve with Seaweed Omelette, p.22, Egg Cups with Paprika, p.31, or Prosciutto and Watercress Spirals, p.59.

---

4 lb (2 kg) broad beans (2 lb/1 kg if shelled)

1 lb (500 g) baby carrots

3 tablespoons walnut or hazelnut oil

salt and freshly ground black pepper

1–2 sprigs fresh savory

• Wear rubber gloves for shelling the beans, or the juice from the pods will blacken your fingers. If the beans are really tiny, leave them raw; otherwise steam for 3–4 minutes. Trim and scrub the carrots (do not peel) and steam them for 3–4 minutes. Toss the oil into the vegetables (leaving the carrots whole). Season to taste and sprinkle the savory leaves on top. Serve at room temperature.

Serves 6

From left to right: *Cherry Consommé (p.66), Tomato and Coconut Soup (p.66), Broad Beans and Baby Carrots with Savory*

Tomato and Coconut Soup

Serve this soup well chilled with hot toast. If giant chives are available, use them for a more pungent flavour.

3–4 large tomatoes

1½ pt (750 ml) stock

1 teaspoon black mustard seeds

4 oz (125 g) desiccated coconut

salt and freshly ground black pepper

1 heaped tablespoon chopped chives

● Immerse the tomatoes in boiling water for 1 minute precisely, then peel and chop roughly. Place the tomatoes, stock and mustard seeds in a saucepan and bring slowly to the boil. Reduce the heat and simmer for 20 minutes. Take off the heat and stir in the coconut. Allow to cool, season, then refrigerate until needed.
● Just before serving, stir in half the chives and decorate the top with the remainder.

Serves 6

Cherry Consommé

This consommé is nice chilled for lunch on a hot day, followed by cucumber and watercress sandwiches cut into mouthful sizes.

---

3 lb (1.5 kg) morello cherries

1½ pt (900 ml) chicken or vegetable stock

juice of ½ lemon

a few chive stems

● Remove the stems from the cherries, cut in half and stone. Reduce to a pulp in a food

processor and add the heated stock until well blended. Stir in the lemon juice and chill until needed. Serve with the chives snipped onto the top.

Serves 6

Leek and Tarama Soup

This combination of leeks and smoked cod's roe works beautifully, resulting in a luscious and intriguing soup. I choose leeks with little green for a more subtle flavour. Serve with brown bread, and perhaps a plain roast chicken with wild rice and courgettes.

---

2 lb (1 kg) large leeks

2 pt (1 litre) chicken stock

4 oz (125 g) smoked cod's roe

¼ pt/5 fl oz (150 ml) double cream

1 teaspoon dried (or 3–4 sprigs fresh) tarragon leaves

freshly ground black pepper

● Trim off and discard most of the green tops of the leeks. Slit lengthways and clean until all the embedded grit is removed. Cut roughly across and place in a large saucepan with the stock. Cover and cook gently for 20 minutes.
● Meanwhile, with a small spoon, remove all the roes from the skin, scraping well to avoid any waste. In a small bowl mash this together with the cream until no lumps remain.
● When the leeks are ready, stir in the tarragon (if fresh tarragon is used, remove the stalks). Allow to cool for 10–15 minutes, then blend well with the smoked cod's roe mixture. Season with pepper only, as the roe's saltiness should be sufficient. Serve the soup chilled or at room temperature.

Serves 6

Potato, Turnip and Radicchio Salad

This is a rather rich salad which goes well with sharp-tasting Citrons Confits, p. 80, or simply with soft-boiled eggs.

---

1 lb (500 g) small new potatoes (Désirée if available)

1 lb (500 g) young turnips

2 tablespoons mayonnaise

¼ pt/5 fl oz (150 ml) sour cream

1–2 dashes Maggi liquid seasoning

salt and freshly ground black pepper

1–2 sprigs fresh (or 1 tablespoon dried) tarragon

1 large or 2 small radicchio heads

● Clean the potatoes and steam for 20 minutes. Meanwhile, trim and peel the turnips and steam for 7–8 minutes. (I do this by adding the turnips to the steaming basket when the potatoes are half cooked, so that both vegetables are ready at the same time.) Allow to cool, and cut the turnips into two.
● Prepare the dressing as follows: in a small bowl beat together the mayonnaise, sour cream and liquid seasoning. Add, sparingly, some salt and freshly milled pepper. Add the whole tarragon leaves, stems removed.
● Shred the radicchio (discard the stem and outer leaves). Toss the cooled potatoes, turnips and radicchio in the dressing. Do not refrigerate this salad as it spoils its flavour. Keep covered, at room temperature, until needed.

Serves 6

Celeriac and Fresh Coriander Soup

This combination of celeriac and fresh coriander works extremely well. Try to get fresh green peppercorns on stalks for this recipe. Otherwise used dried ones. Choose a very smooth celeriac root to avoid waste.

---

1 pt (600 ml) stock

juice of ½ lemon

about 2 sprigs fresh (or 1 tablespoon dried) thyme

1 large celeriac

¼ pt/5 fl oz (150 ml) Greek yoghurt

1 handful fresh coriander leaves

1 heaped teaspoon green peppercorns

celery salt

● Bring the stock to the boil with the lemon juice and thyme (stems removed). Meanwhile, peel and chop the celeriac and immerse it immediately in the boiling liquid to avoid discolouring. Reduce the heat and cook gently for 20 minutes. Blend in a food processor and allow to cool.
● Stir the yoghurt into the mixture until thoroughly blended. Add half the coriander (unchopped, but with stems removed) and the green peppercorns. Season with celery salt. Just before serving decorate with the remaining coriander leaves.

Serves 6

New Potato and Fennel Salad

Small waxy potatoes with thin skins are best for this salad. The fresh-tasting fennel complements the potatoes' blandness. The fresh oregano enhances both flavours.

1½ lb (750 g) small new potatoes (red-skinned if available)

2 medium-sized fennel bulbs

about 4 tablespoons fruity olive oil

salt and freshly ground black pepper

3–4 sprigs fresh (or 1½ tablespoons dried) oregano

• Steam the washed, unpeeled potatoes for 15 minutes. Allow to cool, cut in two and set aside.
• Trim the ends of the fennel and discard the outer leaves if they are stringy or blemished. Then chop roughly, reserving the fronds for decoration.
• Combine the potatoes and fennel in a bowl and toss in the olive oil. Season to taste. Add the whole oregano leaves, stems removed. Transfer to a serving dish, decorate with the reserved fennel fronds and serve.

Serves 6

Clockwise from top: *Celeriac and Fresh Coriander Soup (p.67), Leek and Tarama Soup (p.66), Potato, Turnip and Radicchio Salad (p.67), New Potato and Fennel Salad*

French Beans with Sesame Seeds and Chive Flowers

This dish is excellent with fish or eggs or with the Rabbit and Tongue Terrine, p.60.

---

1 lb (500 g) small French beans

1 teaspoon wine vinegar

1 tablespoon sesame oil

2 tablespoons sunflower oil

1 shallot, finely chopped

salt and freshly ground black pepper

2 oz (60 g) sesame seeds, lightly toasted

2–3 chive flowers

• Snap off the tops of the beans, leaving the tails, and wash them. Steam for 3 minutes, then swiftly rinse under cold running water to preserve their emerald green colour. Set aside.
• Beat together the vinegar and the two oils. Add the shallot and season with salt and pepper. Toss in the French beans, then scatter the sesame seeds over them (they will cling to the coated beans). Lastly sprinkle the chive flowers over the dish.

Serves 6

Cauliflower with Yoghurt and Oregano

Buy a purple cauliflower if available. Although it tastes the same as the white sort, it looks so attractive that it is worth looking out for. I usually use the cauliflower raw, but you could steam it for 2–3 minutes. For a richer dressing, use Greek yoghurt.

---

1 white or purple cauliflower

2 slices white bread, crusts removed

½ pt/10 fl oz (300 ml) plain yoghurt

1 tablespoon fruity olive oil

1 teaspoon soya sauce

3–4 fresh oregano sprigs

salt and freshly ground black pepper

a few borage flowers (optional)

• Wash the cauliflower and pat dry. Cut off the florets and separate them into sprays. Remove the stalks; slice them thinly. Set aside.
• Tear the bread slices into small bits. Spoon some yoghurt over the bread and mash until the bread has absorbed it all. Beat in the remaining yoghurt, along with the olive oil and soya sauce, until well amalgamated. Stir in the sliced cauliflower stalks. Add the oregano leaves, stems removed, and season.
• Arrange the florets in a circular pattern in the serving dish and season with salt and freshly ground pepper. Pile the mixture of yoghurt and stalks in the centre. If you like, you can decorate the dish with borage flowers.

Serves 4–6

Clockwise from right: *Cauliflower with Yoghurt and Oregano, French Beans with Sesame Seeds and Chive Flowers (p. 69), Brussels Sprouts and Raisins with Paprika Mayonnaise*

Brussels Sprouts and Raisins with Paprika Mayonnaise

This mixture of sweet and sour turns a rather ordinary vegetable into an unusual treat. Serve with Turkey Rolls, p. 60, or game.

1½ lb (750 g) Brussels sprouts

1 handful raisins

4 tablespoons mayonnaise

juice of 1 lime

1 teaspoon paprika

1 teaspoon caraway seeds

salt and freshly ground black pepper

• Trim the Brussels sprouts, removing the outer blemished leaves if necessary and steam for 5–6 minutes. Cool under cold running water. If they are large, cut them in two. Pour some boiling water over the raisins and let them soak for 1 or 2 minutes before draining, which makes them softer and plumper.
• Beat together the mayonnaise, lime juice, paprika and caraway seeds. Season to taste. Toss the paprika mayonnaise into the mixture of Brussels sprouts and raisins. Decorate the top with a sprinkling of extra paprika.

Serves 4–6

Beetroot and Celery Salad with Pistachios

This salad combines the contrasting textures of soft beetroot and crunchy celery. The two shades of green, of the celery and pistachios, also contrast nicely with the deep red of the beetroot. Serve with a pasta dish.

4–5 smallish beetroots, freshly cooked

1 celery heart

1 tablespoon tarragon vinegar

2 tablespoons walnut oil

salt and freshly ground black pepper

2 oz (60 g) shelled pistachio nuts

● Peel and chop the beetroot. Clean the celery and slice it thinly. In a bowl, blend together the vinegar and oil and season generously. Toss the celery in the dressing, until just coated, and place on a serving dish. Repeat this procedure with the beetroot until no dressing is left. (This is done in two stages to avoid staining the celery with red beetroot juice.)
● Arrange the beetroot over the celery on the serving dish, and, at the last minute, sprinkle on the roughly chopped pistachios. This salad should not be refrigerated, but kept covered at room temperature until it is served.

Serves 4

Broccoli, Avocado and Red Pepper Salad

This is a very colourful salad with a nice combination of contrasting textures. Serve with a pasta salad, cheese dish or Croissant with Smoked Cod, p. 39.

1½ lb (750 g) broccoli

2 red peppers

2 avocados

1 scant tablespoon tarragon vinegar

1 teaspoon Worcester sauce

about 6 tablespoons olive oil

salt and freshly ground black pepper

2–3 sprigs fresh marjoram or oregano

● Wash and trim the broccoli and steam for 6–8 minutes, depending on size. Cool under cold running water, so that the bright emerald colour is preserved. If any stems are large, split them in halves or quarters.
● With a small knife, remove the stalks, seeds and white inner membranes of the peppers. Slice them thinly. Peel and stone the avocados (do not chop them until the dressing is prepared, to avoid them blackening).
● In a serving bowl beat together the vinegar, Worcester sauce and oil. Season and add the marjoram or oregano leaves, stripped from the stalks. Combine the broccoli, pepper and avocado, cut into chunks. Toss in the dressing and serve.

Serves 6–8

Top: *Beetroot and Celery Salad with Pistachios*
Bottom: *Broccoli, Avocado and Red Pepper Salad*

Cucumber and Raspberry Salad

This is a sophisticated but simple salad to serve in summer when raspberries are at their best. Strawberries and their vinegar can be used instead of raspberries if you prefer. Serve with Savoury Cheese Mille-Feuille, p.35, or Turkey Rolls, p.60, or to accompany any delicate dish.

---

2 cucumbers

salt

1 tablespoon raspberry vinegar

1 punnet raspberries

freshly ground black pepper

1–2 fresh mint sprigs

● Peel the cucumbers and, with a vegetable peeler, cut lengthways, into thin ribbons. Place in a colander and sprinkle with salt. Allow the cucumbers to disgorge for at least 2 hours, then pat dry. Toss with the vinegar and arrange, loosely curled, in a serving dish. Scatter in the raspberries and season the dish generously with pepper. Tuck whole mint leaves amongst the cucumber ribbons and raspberries. Chill before serving.

Serves 4

Squash and Radish Salad

Summer squash has a taste similar to courgettes. In this recipe it is used raw. Squash comes in various shapes and colours, but try to buy the yellow ones, streaked with green and white, and with scalloped edges. These ingredients make a crunchy salad which goes well with soft-textured dishes, such as Scrambled Eggs with Radicchio, p.12, or the Rigatoni, Smoked Chicken and Mango, p.8, or Tomato and Ricotta Roulade, p.20.

---

3 small squashes

1 bunch radishes with leaves

juice of ½ lemon

2 tablespoons hazelnut or walnut oil

salt and freshly ground black pepper

1 tablespoon chopped chives

● Wash the squashes and cut thinly across in order to show the pretty shape. Small squashes shouldn't need to have seeds removed as they aren't yet properly formed. Wash the radishes, pat dry and cut in thin slices. Wash the radish leaves thoroughly, so that all grit is removed. Steam for 3 minutes and refresh under cold running water. Squeeze dry and chop finely.
● In a small bowl, beat together the lemon juice and nut oil. Season to taste. Place the squash and radish slices on a serving dish, piling the radish leaves in the centre. Pour over the dressing and scatter the chives evenly on top.

Serves 4–6

Top: *Cucumber and Raspberry Salad*
Bottom: *Squash and Radish Salad*

Petits-Pois Mould

This recipe goes well with fish. It would make an excellent accompaniment for Plaice with Walnut and Paprika Sauce, p.49, or Marinated Scallops and Fried Seaweed, p.40.

---

1 lb (500 g) frozen minted petits-pois

2 slices of white bread, crusts removed

2 tablespoons milk

2 oz (60 g) butter, just melted

3 large eggs

salt and freshly ground black pepper

1–2 fresh mint sprigs

A Pour some boiling water over the peas and leave for 5 minutes, then drain. Soak the bread in the milk. Place both in a food processor and reduce to a purée. Add the butter and egg yolks. Season with salt and pepper. Blend well. Whisk the egg whites until firm, but not stiff, and fold into the pea mixture. Pour into a greased pudding basin (the basin should be only three-quarters filled), but do not cover it. Lower into a pan of boiling water, so that the water comes halfway up the basin. Cover the pan and steam for 1 hour. Allow to cool and turn out onto a dish. Serve decorated with the mint sprigs.

Serves 4–6

Variation: Replace the green peas with yellow or green courgettes.

Okra, Bacon and Ginger Salad

The crunchy bacon contrasts nicely with the okra's delicate, slightly gelatinous texture. This dish is excellent with Leek Shortcake, p.30, and Ham and Water Chestnut Parcels, p.59. You could also try it with Lentils with Yoghurt and Raw Spinach Sauce, p.28, or Rainbow Trout in Filo Pastry, p.50.

---

5 bacon slices

1 lb (500 g) okra

2 in (5 cm) fresh ginger root

1 generous tablespoon sesame oil

juice of ½ lime

salt and freshly ground black pepper

• Fry the bacon, without using any extra fat, until it is brown and crispy. Drain on kitchen paper.
• Pare off the okra stalks without cutting into the pods. Wash and pat dry. Steam for 3 to 4 minutes and cool under cold running water. Set aside.
• Peel and cut the ginger into julienne strips. Stir into the sesame oil and add the lime juice. Season with salt and pepper. Transfer to a serving dish and crumble the bacon on top.

Serves 4–6

Top: *Petit-Pois Mould*
Bottom: *Okra, Bacon and Ginger Salad*

Courgette and Leek Salad with Sage

Courgettes and leeks complement each other nicely, and the crunchy, fried sage leaves add an intriguing note to the salad. Serve with Rice and Parmesan Salad, p.11, and Ham and Water Chestnut Parcels, p.59.

---

4 medium-sized courgettes

3 medium-sized leeks

1 teaspoon strong French mustard

salt and freshly ground black pepper

2 teaspoons tarragon vinegar

4–5 tablespoons walnut oil

about 10 fresh sage leaves

oil for frying

1 hard-boiled egg, finely chopped

● Wash, trim and pat dry the courgettes, then cut across in half and set aside. Remove most of the green part of the leeks and discard the outer leaves. Clean them scrupulously until all the grit is removed. Drain and cut across into thirds. Steam the leeks for 8 minutes and the courgettes for 5 minutes. Allow to cool.
● To make the dressing beat the mustard, salt, pepper and vinegar together with a fork. Then add the oil in a stream, beating constantly until it emulsifies and the oil is incorporated.
● Fry the sage leaves until crisp and drain on kitchen paper. Place the sliced vegetables on a serving dish, pour on the vinaigrette and scatter the chopped egg on top. Lastly decorate with the sage leaves.

Serves 6

Radicchio, Bean Shoot and Mint Salad

In this dish the slight bitterness of the radicchio contrasts nicely with the fresh-tasting mint. The dressing's ingredients impart a somewhat Chinese note to the salad. Buy the bean shoots fresh on the day you want to make the salad as they tend to discolour very quickly.

---

3 medium-sized radicchio heads

1 lb (500 g) bean shoots

6–8 fresh mint sprigs

juice of 1 lemon

2 tablespoons soya sauce

3–4 tablespoons sesame oil

salt and freshly ground black pepper

● Trim the radicchio, discarding any blemished or wilted leaves. Separate and tear each leaf in half, and place them in a bowl with the bean shoots (green shoots removed if wanted). Clean and dry the mint sprigs, pluck off the leaves and add them, whole, to the salad. Cover the bowl with a damp cloth or cling film and refrigerate until needed.
● For the dressing, beat together the lemon juice, soya sauce and sesame oil in a small bowl. Season to taste. Just before serving gently mix the dressing into the salad.

Serves 4–6

Variation: If you like, you can replace the sesame oil with grape-seed oil for a lighter flavour.

Top: *Radicchio, Bean Shoot and Mint Salad*
Bottom: *Courgette and Leek Salad with Sage*

Citrons Confits

These are pickled lemons (a recipe which originated in North Africa). I serve them either added to a rice or tomato salad or with a chicken dish. Choose lemons without any blemishes.

---

6 lemons

6 teaspoons coarse sea salt

about 10 coriander seeds (optional)

1 bay leaf

2 sprigs fresh (or 1 tablespoon dried) thyme

3 garlic cloves, peeled

1 teaspoon vegetable oil

● Immerse the whole lemons in boiling water for 10 seconds. Drain and wipe to remove any traces of preservative, then rinse and pat dry. Cut each lemon in four, leaving the quarters still joined at the base. Fill each centre with 1 teaspoon coarse sea salt and put the lemons in a scrupulously clean jar, adding the coriander seeds (if used), bay leaf, thyme and garlic. Cover with warm water and add the oil. Keep in a cool place and wait a minimum of 15 days before eating. (But pickled lemons improve if left for 1 or 2 months). Serve thinly sliced across with vegetables, salads or chicken.

Makes 6

Marinated Courgettes with Mint

This dish may be prepared in advance and kept for several days. After a day or so the courgettes become more refreshing and the sharpness of the vinegar mellows. Serve with cold meat or poultry.

---

8 small courgettes

¼ pt (150 ml) fruity olive oil

1 garlic clove, peeled and finely chopped

3–4 sprigs fresh mint leaves, stripped off their stalks

salt and freshly ground black pepper

¼ pt (150 ml) wine vinegar

● Slice the courgettes lengthways into four. Heat the oil in a sauté pan and cook the courgette slices, one layer at a time, until both sides are golden. With a perforated spoon, remove and drain the slices (returning the drippings to the sauté pan).
● Transfer the courgettes to a straight-sided, shallow serving dish. Combine the garlic and freshly shredded mint leaves in a small bowl and sprinkle them over the courgettes. Season with salt and freshly ground black pepper. In a small saucepan, bring the vinegar to a boil and pour it over the courgettes immediately. Allow to cool. Cover and marinate, refrigerated, for at least 12 hours.

Serves 6–8

Clockwise from right: *Citrons Confits, Shredded Radicchio (p. 82), Marinated Courgettes with Mint, Lettuce Purée (p. 82)*

Lettuce Purée

This versatile purée can be served as a side dish with game or poultry, or perhaps with two soft-boiled eggs nested in the centre. It can also be thinned down with stock for a soup.

---

4 lettuces

½ pt/10 fl oz (300 ml) sour cream or smetana

nutmeg

salt and freshly ground black pepper

● Trim the base of each lettuce and discard any blemished leaves. Wash, dry and chop roughly. Purée in a food processor, turning the motor on and off. Add the sour cream (or smetana), a few nutmeg gratings and season with salt and freshly ground black pepper. Process again for 1 or 2 seconds, or until just bound. Check the seasoning and adjust accordingly. Transfer the purée to a dish and serve.

Serves 3–4

Shredded Radicchio

This salad looks very attractive, dotted with red, white and green. Serve it with steamed fish, game or poultry.

---

3 medium-sized radicchio heads

1 bunch flat-leaved parsley, chopped

¼ pt/5 fl oz (150 ml) yoghurt or buttermilk

2 tablespoons mayonnaise

juice of ½ lime

salt and freshly ground black pepper

● Cut off the stems of the radicchio and any wilted outer leaves. Wash, pat dry, and then shred finely. Mix in a bowl with the parsley. Stir in the yoghurt (or buttermilk), mayonnaise and lime juice. Season to taste and serve.

Serves 2–4

Okra and Coconut

It is important to pick small, unblemished okra for this dish as larger ones tend to be stringy. I buy creamed coconut in a solid block, ready to be melted for use.

---

2 oz (60 g) large coconut flakes

1 oz (30 g) butter, melted

salt and freshly ground black pepper

1 lb (500 g) small okra

4 oz (125 g) creamed coconut

¼ pt (150 ml) stock

• Preheat the oven to 375°F/190°C/Gas 5. Toss the coconut flakes into the melted butter and season. Spread on an oven sheet and bake for 10 minutes or until golden. Reserve.
• Pare off the okra stalks without cutting into the pods. Wash and pat dry. Steam for 4–5 minutes. Rinse under cold running water. Set aside.
• In a heavy saucepan, heat the creamed coconut and stock, stirring constantly until the coconut is completely dissolved. Season and allow to cool.
• Toss the coconut mixture with the okra and transfer to a serving dish. Just before serving, scatter the coconut flakes on top.

Serves 4–6

Asparagus and Carrot Salad with Pine Nuts

A crunchy, light salad to serve on a hot day with a pasta dish or Prosciutto and Watercress Spirals, p.59.

---

1 lb (500 g) baby carrots

1 lb (500 g) thin asparagus

2 tablespoons walnut oil

juice of ½ lemon

salt and freshly ground black pepper

about 10 fresh basil leaves

2 oz (60 g) pine nuts, lightly toasted

• Scrub the carrots (for young carrots peeling is unnecessary), trim the asparagus and cut each stalk into three lengths. Steam for 6–7 minutes. Allow to cool. Cut the asparagus again into broad slices and the carrots in two lengthways.
• Beat together the walnut oil and lemon juice and season. Toss this mixture with the vegetables. Serve with basil leaves, torn into small pieces, and the pine nuts scattered on top.

Serves 6

Spinach with Anchovies and Tofu

The flavour of anchovies is somehow toned down here, giving a lovely, intriguing tang to the spinach. The bland tofu is a good complement in texture to the other ingredients. Serve with fried triangle-shaped croûtons and any egg dish.

---

2 lb (1 kg) fresh spinach

2 pieces tofu, cubed

2 tablespoons fruity olive oil

1 × 2 oz (50 g) tin anchovy fillets, drained and finely chopped

1 garlic clove, finely chopped

freshly ground black pepper

juice and grated rind of 1 lime

• Wash the spinach thoroughly and remove the stems. Drain, leaving some water clinging to the leaves. Marinate the tofu in 1 tablespoon of olive oil while you cook the spinach. In a large saucepan heat the remaining oil with the anchovy fillets and garlic, until the fillets dissolve. Add all the spinach and cover. Cook for 4–5 minutes, tossing once or twice while cooking (the leaves should be wilted but still a bright green colour). Transfer immediately to a serving dish, adding the tofu and a generous amount of pepper. Sprinkle on the lime juice and scatter the rind on top.
• Serve at room temperature.

Serves 6

Clockwise from top: *Spinach with Anchovies and Tofu, Asparagus and Carrot Salad with Pine Nuts (p. 83), Okra and Coconut (p. 83)*

Chinese Salad

This salad is quickly made, as it uses mainly tinned ingredients. The only secret lies in a lazy Chinese-style inspiration. All the ingredients are normally available in supermarkets.

---

1 lb (500 g) small okra

1 carambola (or star) fruit

1 packet (about 3½ oz/100 g) shiitake mushrooms or 4 oz (125 g) button mushrooms

1 × 8 oz (250 g) tin water chestnuts

1 × 15 oz (430 g) tin artichoke hearts

1 × 15 oz (430 g) tin baby corn

1 × 8 oz (250 g) tin kidney beans

1 handful flat-leaved parsley, coarsely chopped

2 teaspoons soya sauce

juice of 1½ lemons

4–5 tablespoons sesame oil

1 sprig fresh green peppercorns or 1 scant tablespoon dried green peppercorns

---

• Pare off the okra stalks without cutting into the pods. Wash and steam for 3 minutes. Swiftly refresh under cold running water. Pare the tough ridges off the carambola and slice thinly across, revealing its pretty star-like shape.
• Drain off the juice from all the tinned ingredients. Cut the water chestnuts and artichoke hearts into two to four pieces (depending on size), and the baby corn in two (if necessary). Trim and cut the button mushrooms, if using, into quarters. Add the other ingredients.
• Make the dressing, beating together the soya sauce, lemon juice and sesame oil. Add the green peppercorns, removed from the stalk (or the dried peppercorns, lightly crushed). Toss the dressing into all the ingredients.

Serves 6–8

Baby Artichokes and Cherry Tomatoes

I buy tiny globe artichokes for this dish, dressed in a mustardy vinaigrette. Serve with a pasta dish and Veal and Pistachio, p.56, or Ham and Water Chestnut Parcels, p.59.

---

2 lb (1 kg) baby globe artichokes

1 lb (500 g) cherry tomatoes

1 heaped teaspoon strong French mustard

salt and freshly ground black pepper

juice of ½ lemon

about 6 tablespoons fruity olive oil

a few chive blades

• Wash and dry the artichokes. Remove the stalks. Cut in half, remove the outer leaves and steam for 8–10 minutes. Set aside. Wash the tomatoes, pat dry and remove the calyces. Cut them into two.
• Make a vinaigrette as follows: in a small bowl, beat the mustard, salt and pepper and the lemon juice with a fork. Add the olive oil in a stream, as you would for a mayonnaise. You should then have a thick, emulsified dressing. Check the seasoning and adjust if necessary.
• To serve, mix the vinaigrette into the combined artichokes and tomatoes and snip the chives over the top.

Serves 6

Mange-Touts and Carrots with Stilton Sauce

This rich, velvety sauce nicely complements the crunchy-textured mange-touts and carrots. Try to buy small carrots in bunches as they are sweeter. The mange-touts may be replaced with lightly steamed spinach. Serve with rice or new potatoes.

---

1 lb (500 g) mange-touts

about 2 lb (1 kg) smallish carrots

½ lb (250 g) white Stilton cheese

about ½ pt/10 fl oz (300 ml) Greek yoghurt or thick cream

1 scant teaspoon caraway seeds

salt

1 heaped teaspoon fresh or dry green peppercorns, lightly crushed, or cayenne pepper

---

• Remove the tails from the mange-touts and steam for 3 minutes. Rinse under cold running water. Trim and scrub the carrots, cut them in two lengthways and steam for 15 minutes. Allow them to cool and then slice thinly.
• If necessary remove the rind, and then mash the Stilton with a fork. Add the yoghurt (or cream) little by little, making a smooth paste. Stir in the caraway seeds and season with salt and green peppercorns (or cayenne pepper).
• Arrange the mange-touts around the rim of the serving dish, with the carrots inside. Pile the sauce in the centre and serve.

Serves 6

Clockwise from top: *Mange-Touts and Carrots with Stilton Sauce, Baby Artichokes and Cherry Tomatoes, Chinese Salad (p.85)*

Avocado Ice

This is a savoury ice, rather rich tasting and unusual. The fragrant basil goes well with the bland taste of the avocado. Nasturtiums – if used – add a peppery taste as well as a touch of colour.

2–3 ripe avocados

¼ pt (150 ml) mayonnaise

¼ pt/5 fl oz (150 ml) sour cream or yoghurt

juice of 1 lemon

1 teaspoon soya sauce

salt and freshly ground black pepper

about 30 fresh basil leaves

nasturtium flowers (optional)

• Stone and peel the avocados and blend throughly with the mayonnaise, sour cream (or yoghurt), lemon juice and soya sauce. Season to taste and stir in the torn basil leaves (perhaps reserving a few for decoration if the nasturtium flowers are not used).
• Pour the mixture into a 1 pt (600 ml) ring mould and freeze. An hour before serving transfer to the refrigerator to let the ice soften.
• Turn out and serve decorated with nasturtium flowers or basil leaves.

Serves 8–10

Avocado, Cranberry and Orange Salad

In this recipe textures and flavours contrast intriguingly: smooth, bland avocado with juicy, sharp cranberry and orange. The array of colours also makes this salad very appealing. Serve with Savoury Cheese Mille-Feuille, p.35, or Quails' Eggs en Gelée, p.14.

½ lb (250 g) cranberries

2 oranges

3 ripe avocados

juice of 1 lemon

1 teaspoon honey

2 tablespoons olive oil

½ bunch watercress

salt and freshly ground black pepper

• In a saucepan, bring to the boil about ½ pt (300 ml) of water. Add the cranberries, lower the heat to simmering point and cook for 4–5 minutes. Drain and reserve. Peel and slice the oranges. Reserve any excess juice for the dressing. Peel the avocados and cut them in two. Then remove the stones and then cut the flesh into medium-sized pieces.
• Beat the lemon juice, reserved orange juice, honey and olive oil together. Add the watercress, finely chopped. Season with salt and pepper. Pour the dressing into a bowl in which you have combined the cranberries, oranges and avocados. As the salad cools, the flavours will combine.

Serves 6

Top: *Avocado Ice* Bottom: *Avocado, Cranberry and Orange Salad*

Yellow Peppers with Spinach

This is a simple, colourful dish. As it is light, you can serve it with a rich one such as Rice and Parmesan Salad, p.11. The spinach may be replaced with Swiss chard.

---

6 smallish yellow peppers

about 2¾ lb (1.25 kg) fresh spinach

1 generous tablespoon fruity olive oil

grated nutmeg or mace

salt and freshly ground black pepper

• Cut off a slice from the tops of the peppers. Carefully remove the seeds and inner white membranes.
• Wash the spinach thoroughly. Cut off the stems and drain, but do not dry it. Some water should still cling to the leaves. In a large saucepan, slowly heat half the oil and add half the spinach. Increase the heat and cover. Leave to cook for about 3 minutes, turning and tossing the wilted leaves with a wooden spoon until reduced by half. Remove the spinach from the pan and set aside. Empty out the liquid left in the bottom of the pan and, without cleaning it, add the remaining oil and repeat the procedure with the rest of the spinach. Season with nutmeg (or mace), salt and pepper.
• When the spinach is cold, pile it inside the peppers until they are generously filled.

Serves 6

Red Peppers with Ham and Kidney Beans

This dish can be prepared quickly and has an attractive array of colours. You may replace the ham with leftover poultry or game. Serve with an egg dish and a vegetable salad.

---

4 medium-sized red peppers

4 oz (125 g) cooked ham

10 oz (250 g) kidney beans, cooked

¼ pt/5 fl oz (150 ml) sour cream

a few sprigs fresh dill, finely chopped

salt and freshly ground black pepper

• Cut off a slice from the top of each of the peppers to form a lid. Discard the seeds and remove the inner white membranes, taking care not to break through the skins. Chop the ham and place it in a bowl with the kidney beans. Stir in the cream and dill and season.
• Spoon the filling into the prepared peppers. Replace the lids and serve. (The peppers may be halved lengthways, but if you serve them that way you will need a little more filling for each one.)

Serves 4

Top: *Yellow Peppers with Spinach*
Bottom: *Red Peppers with Ham and Kidney Beans*

91

Mushrooms with Aubergines

In this recipe the aubergines are steamed, thus avoiding the heavy absorption of fat caused by frying. The combination of mushrooms and aubergines turn this simple dish into a luscious treat. If available, use oyster mushrooms, which are available in larger supermarkets.

---

2 medium-sized aubergines

½ lb (250 g) mushrooms

2 slices wholemeal bread

1 garlic clove

salt and freshly ground black pepper

a few leaves of fresh thyme

1 oz (30 g) Parmesan cheese, freshly grated

● Wipe the aubergines clean and trim off the tops and bottoms. Do not peel, but slice thinly. Steam for 8 minutes, or until the flesh is a little translucent and soft. Allow to cool.
● Wipe the mushrooms clean and trim off the stalks. Steam for 5 minutes. Meanwhile, toast the bread slices to a rather dark golden colour and leave until quite dry. Rub all over with the garlic. Cut the bread into long slivers or sticks.
● To assemble, place the mushrooms in one layer in a serving dish. Season. Scatter the thyme and some of the Parmesan on top. Cover the mushrooms with the aubergine slices, slightly overlapping. Season. Sprinkle with the remaining Parmesan. Surround with the bread sticks placed upright.

Serves 4

Aubergine Flan with Coriander

This combination of aubergine and coriander is delicious. Although the dish tastes rich, the fact that the aubergines are baked, rather than fried, keeps it light. Serve with a green salad and smoked turkey.

---

3 large aubergines

1 lb (500 g) cottage cheese

3 eggs, beaten

1 garlic clove, finely chopped

2 oz (60 g) Parmesan cheese, freshly grated

a handful fresh coriander, chopped

salt and freshly ground black pepper

● Wrap the aubergines in foil and bake in a medium oven (350°F/180°C/Gas 4) for 45 minutes. Allow to cool for 5 minutes, unwrap and slit lengthways with a sharp knife. Scoop out all the flesh with a spoon and place it in a bowl, reserving the skins.
● Raise the oven temperature to 400°F/200°C/Gas 6. Add the cottage cheese to the aubergine pulp, along with the eggs, garlic, Parmesan and fresh coriander. Season well. Line a greased 1¼ pt (750 ml) charlotte mould with the flattened aubergine skins. Fill with the aubergine mixture and fold over any protruding edges of the skins. Bake in a bain-marie for 45 minutes or until done. Prick the centre with a skewer: it should come out clean. If it does not, switch off the oven and leave the flan for 5–7 minutes longer. Remove and let it cool in the mould. Just before serving unmould onto a serving dish.

Serves 6

Top: *Aubergine Flan with Coriander*
Bottom: *Mushrooms with Aubergines*

Savoury Baked Apples

These apples are filled with rice, ham and herbs. For a change, replace the turmeric with saffron or curry powder. Serve with game or poultry.

6 Red or Golden Delicious apples

1 lb (500 g) cooked rice

4 oz (125g) cooked ham, finely chopped

1 teaspoon crumbled dried sage leaves (or 6–7 shredded fresh leaves)

½ teaspoon fresh or dried thyme

2 oz (60g) currants

3 tablespoons fruity olive oil

3 oz (90g) peeled walnuts, chopped

salt and freshly ground black pepper

½ teaspoon turmeric

● Preheat the oven to 375°F/190°C/Gas 5. Cut off the top ½in (1 cm) of the apples and core them. Using a melon-ball cutter, scoop out and reserve the flesh, leaving a thickish shell.
● In a bowl, combine the rice, ham, sage, thyme, currants, olive oil and walnuts. Add the apple flesh, chopped. Season to taste with salt, pepper and turmeric. Divide the stuffing among the apple shells, packing it into mounds. Place the apples in a baking pan. Pour in 1 in (2.5 cm) of hot water and bake the apples, tightly covered with foil, in the preheated oven for about 1½ hours, or until just tender.
● Let cool and transfer to a serving dish decorated with more sage if desired.

Serves 6

Top: *Filled Globe Artichokes*
Bottom: *Savoury Baked Apples*

Filled Globe Artichokes

The artichokes are filled with a lemony tomato stuffing thickened with bread. (Use a good quality French or Italian bread for this.) Serve with Rabbit and Tongue Terrine, p.60, or Radicchio, Bean Shoot and Mint Salad, p.79.

4 globe artichokes

2 lemons

½–¾ loaf of bread, 1 day old

1 large tomato, peeled and chopped

a few garlic shavings

1½ tablespoons fruity olive oil

sea salt

freshly ground black pepper

● Remove the tough outer leaves and trim the stems of the artichokes. Rub the remainder with a lemon half to keep them from discolouring. Drop the artichokes into a saucepan of boiling salted water into which you have squeezed the juice and added the peel of one lemon. Cook for 20–25 minutes, depending on the size of the artichokes. They are ready when a leaf can be pulled away easily. Drain and plunge swiftly into a bowl of iced water. Allow to cool thoroughly. Invert on kitchen paper to drain further.
● Remove the crust from the bread and tear the remainder into pieces. Soak in 5 tablespoons of water for a few minutes, then squeeze dry. Place the prepared bread in a bowl with the juice and grated rind of the second lemon, the chopped tomato, garlic shavings and olive oil. Combine all the ingredients well and season.
● Remove the fuzzy 'chokes' from the artichokes – the easiest way of doing this is first to cut them lengthwise. Spread out the leaves. Spoon some of the filling into the cavity left by the choke and more between the outer leaves. Eat the filling using the artichoke leaves as scoops.

Serves 4 or 8

Baby Corn and Broad Beans with Basil and Poppy Seeds

It is quite easy to find fresh baby corn. The little cobs are about the size of a finger. For this recipe buy already shelled broad beans. The poppy seeds add a delicate nutty flavour and speckle the dish with tiny bluish-purple dots. Serve with Rainbow Trout in Filo Pastry, p.50, or Rabbit and Tongue Terrine, p.60.

1 lb (500 g) packet fresh baby corn

1 lb (500 g) packet shelled broad beans

¼ pt/5 fl oz (150 ml) sour cream

about 10 fresh basil leaves

salt and freshly ground black pepper

2–3 gratings of nutmeg

1 heaped teaspoon poppy seeds

● Steam the corn for 4–5 minutes, let cool a little and cut into broad slices. Steam the broad beans for 6–7 minutes, then, while still warm, pinch open the seam and remove the beans from their skins, which should be discarded.
● Beat the sour cream with the torn basil leaves and season with salt, pepper and nutmeg. Stir the creamy sauce into the cool vegetables. Scatter the poppy seeds on top.

Serves 4

Watercress Mousse with Avocado

I find that the peppery taste of the watercress in this recipe pleasantly counteracts the blandness of the avocado. Serve, if you like, with Tomato and Parsley Sauce, p.20, and croûtons.

4 oz (125 g) cream cheese

¼ pt/5 fl oz (150 ml) sour cream

2 hard-boiled eggs

¼ pt (150 ml) chicken stock

1 packet (½ oz/12 g) gelatine

3 bunches watercress

juice of 1 lemon

2 avocados

salt and white pepper

● Beat the cream cheese with the sour cream until smooth. Chop the eggs finely and add them to the creamy mixture. Heat, but do not boil, the stock, then sprinkle the gelatine over it. Stir until dissolved. Allow to cool.
● Cut off the watercress stems and discard any blemished or yellowed leaves. Chop it finely (reserving a few sprigs for decoration). Stir the watercress and lemon juice and cooled stock mixture into the cream mixture and adjust the seasoning to taste. Then transfer either into a wetted large savarin mould (8 in/20 cm) or into six individual ramekins and chill.
● Just before serving, invert in the centre of a round flat dish and shake gently to loosen. Remove the mould. Stone and peel the avocados and slice them lengthways. Arrange them round the outer rim of the dish so that they frame the mousse. Decorate with the reserved watercress leaves.

Serves 6

Top: *Baby Corn and Broad Beans with Basil and Poppy Seeds* Bottom: *Watercress Mousse with Avocado*

Kidney Bean and Carrot Cake

This is in fact a vegetable mould, wrapped in spinach leaves and served with fiery horse-radish sauce. It would go well with Leek Short-cake, p.30, or Croissant with Smoked Cod, p.39.

1 lb (500 g) fresh spinach

2 lb (1 kg) carrots

2 packets (1 oz/25 g) powdered gelatine

juice of 1½ lemons

1 heaped teaspoon caraway seeds

3 tablespoons sesame oil

2 tablespoons sunflower oil

2 teaspoons strong French mustard

a few gratings of nutmeg

celery salt

freshly ground black pepper

1 × 15 oz (425 g) tin kidney beans

For the sauce

8 fl oz (250 ml) sour cream

1 tablespoon horseradish sauce

cayenne pepper

salt

● Wash the spinach until thoroughly clean. Remove the stalks and steam for 1 minute or until the leaves become limp but still retain their bright green colour. Cool under cold running water. Pat dry and reserve.
● Peel the carrots and cut them into two or three pieces. Steam or boil for 15–20 minutes or until tender. Meanwhile, line a 9–10 in (23–25 cm) china flan dish with two-thirds of the whole spinach leaves, laid so that they overlap the edges.

Top: *Kidney Beans and Carrot Cake*
Bottom: *Belgian Endive with Cheese and Dill*

● Dissolve the gelatine in the lemon juice over a gentle heat. In a food processor, purée the cooked carrots. Then stir in the gelatine along with the caraway seeds, sesame and sunflower oils, mustard and nutmeg. Season adequately with celery salt and freshly ground pepper. Allow to cool.
● Rinse and drain the kidney beans. Spoon half the carrot purée onto the spinach casing and smooth it over evenly. Scatter the kidney beans on top. Cover with the remaining carrot purée and cover with the overlapping spinach leaves. Conceal the filling with the reserved spinach leaves. Brush with a little extra oil, cover with foil and refrigerate for at least 6 hours or, better, overnight.
● Turn out onto a serving dish and brush over with oil for a shiny effect. Cut in nice, neat wedges with a serrated knife. Mix all the ingredients of the sauce and serve separately.

Serves 6–8

Belgian Endive with Cheese and Dill

This works well for a buffet or a pre-meal snack.

3–4 Belgian endives

about ½ lb (250 g) Wensleydale or other moist, crumbly cheese

freshly ground black pepper

a few fresh dill sprigs

● Trim off a little of the base of each endive and separate the leaves carefully. Pile some cheese in each scoop. Season with pepper and place a small dill sprig on top. Arrange prettily in a basket or on a shallow dish.

Serves 4–8

Berry and Grape Tart

Here the pastry is baked blind and the fruit is embedded in an almond-flavoured filling afterwards, so preserving its delicate appearance. If you like, serve with extra sour cream, flavoured with a little cinnamon.

8 oz (250 g) shortcrust pastry

sugar to sprinkle on pastry

—————— *Filling:* ——————

1 tablespoon cornflour

½ pt/10 fl oz (300 ml) sour cream

1 egg, lightly beaten

3 tablespoons caster sugar

1 oz (30 g) butter

4 oz (125 g) ground almonds

grated zest of 1 lime

1 punnet blackberries

1 punnet blueberries or raspberries

1 lb (500 g) seedless grapes

- Preheat the oven to 400°F/200°C/Gas 6.
- Roll out the pastry and leave it for a few minutes before lining an 8 in (20 cm) tin. Crimp the edges. Cover with foil and weight down with dried beans. Bake for 20–25 minutes or until lightly browned.
- Meanwhile, make the filling. Mix the cornflour with a little sour cream in a little saucepan. Add the beaten egg, sugar, butter, ground almonds, lime zest and the remaining sour cream. Bring slowly to the boil, stirring constantly until the mixture thickens. Remove from the heat and allow to cool, stirring from time to time to prevent a skin from forming.
- Sprinkle the bottom of the hot pastry case with sugar. Leave to cool and then spread in the filling mixture. Arrange the berries on it, then the grapes. Serve at room temperature.

Serves 6–8

Nectarines with Frangipane and Grand Marnier

The combination of nectarines and almond-flavoured frangipane turns this simple dessert into a delicate-tasting treat. You may replace the nectarines with fragrant white peaches.

6 nectarines

3 oz (100 g) caster sugar

3 oz (100 g) unsalted butter

3 oz (100 g) ground almonds

2 eggs, separated

2 tablespoons Grand Marnier

½ tablespoon demerara sugar

- Wash the nectarines and pat dry. Cut around each fruit lengthways, then, holding it gently in your hands, twist the two halves first to the left and then to the right, so easing them apart. Separate and remove the stone. Repeat the operation with the other nectarines.
- To make the frangipane, cream the sugar and butter until fluffy and a pale straw colour. Add the ground almonds, then the lightly beaten egg yolks. Beat constantly, making sure that the mixture stays smooth. Stir in the liqueur. Beat the egg whites and demerara sugar into soft peaks.
- Pile a little of the frangipane inside the hollows of the nectarines. Cover with some of the egg whites, spreading with a large fork so as to leave ridges in the whites. Place the prepared nectarines on a lined metal tray and brown under a grill until golden. (This should take 1 minute at the most.) Allow to cool, then serve. The nectarines should be filled only a few hours in advance.

Serves 6

Top: *Berry and Grape Tart*
Bottom: *Nectarines with Frangipane and Grand Marnier*

Strawberries with Claret

This very simple dessert is fit for a king if you use a good vintage claret.

---

1 lb (500 g) strawberries, hulled

½ bottle claret

2 tablespoons sugar (optional)

● Divide the strawberries into four glasses. Pour some of the wine over each. Leave to marinate for at least 1 hour. Eat with a spoon straight from the glass, sprinkling a little sugar on top if you like.

Serves 4

Kumquat Compôte

Kumquats are oval-shaped, small citrus fruits, about 1 in (2.5 cm) long, with edible skins. They are juicy and tart, but have a mellow fragrance when poached. If you like, serve in the Ice Bowl, p. 104.

¼ pt (125 ml) water

4 oz (125 g) sugar

1 lb (500 g) kumquats

● Make a syrup with the water and sugar, and bring slowly to the boil until the liquid is transparent. Reduce the heat and add the whole kumquats. Simmer for 20 minutes, then allow to cool. Serve chilled in hot weather, otherwise at room temperature.

Serves 4

Left: *Kumquat Compôte*
Right: *Strawberries with Claret*

Ice Bowl

This bowl is made of ice and looks quite spectacular when brought to the table. It has the appearance of carved rock crystal. I use it as a container for Kumquat Compôte, p.103, or for fruit salad or sorbet.

● Half fill a mixing bowl (a stainless steel or plastic one works best for this) with water. Float a smaller bowl inside, weighing it down so that the cavity it creates will form a container of the size you will need (old-fashioned scale weights wrapped in plastic work well). Secure the bowls together with a little tape, making sure that the inner one is properly centred (otherwise it tends to float to one side). Then place flat in the freezer.

● Leave until the water is throughly frozen. Remove from the freezer and leave for about 5–7 minutes before removing the inner bowl. Then run some water under the larger bowl until the outer bowl can be removed easily. Wrap the ice bowl in foil or plastic and replace in the freezer until required.

Right: *Ice Bowl*

Japanese Sorbet

I use Japanese plum wine to flavour this sorbet, which somehow doesn't taste sweet. It would be nice served with Caramelized Plums, p.114.

---

4 oz (125 g) sugar

½ pt (300 ml) water

1 stick cinnamon bark

7 fl oz (200 ml) plum wine

1 egg white

2 oz (60 g) caster sugar

● Slowly bring to the boil the 4 oz (125 g) sugar and water with the cinnamon. Cool and strain. Add the plum wine and freeze.
● When the mixture is partly frozen and mushy, beat the egg white stiffly, and, still beating, add the caster sugar. Lighly beat the frozen mixture and fold in the egg white. Freeze again. Serve straight from the freezer (the sorbet softens quickly because of the quantity of alcohol in it) in chilled, frosted glasses. Stir the sorbet lightly with a fork before putting it into the glasses.

Serves 6

Lychee Sorbet

This has a clear taste which refreshes the palate nicely, particularly at the end of a rich, spicy meal.

1¼ lb (570 g) tinned lychees in syrup

3 oz (90 g) sugar

juice of ½ lemon

● Drain the syrup from the lychees and put it in a heavy saucepan with the sugar. Bring slowly to the boil, stirring until the sugar is dissolved. Set aside and allow to cool, then stir in the lemon juice.
● Place the lychees in a food processor and reduce to a pulp (do not worry if little bits are left). With the motor still running, pour in the cooled syrup. Transfer to an ice tray and freeze the mixture for 2 hours or until mushy. Beat vigorously to break up the ice crystals and refreeze. Transfer to the refrigerator 1 hour before serving to allow the sorbet to soften a little.

Serves 6

Top: *Lychee Sorbet*
Bottom: *Japanese Sorbet*

Rice and Coconut Pudding with Lychees

This pudding, with its several shades of white, looks quite beautiful and simple. It would be a good idea to serve this with fresh lychees, unpeeled, piled in a basket.

3 oz (90 g) pudding rice

1 pt (600 ml) full-cream milk

1 vanilla pod, split open

2–3 tablespoons caster sugar

2 tablespoons unsweetened desiccated coconut

1 tablespoon rum

½ pt/10 fl oz (300 ml) sour cream

1¼ lb (570 g) tinned lychees in syrup

● I use a double boiler for this recipe. Place the rice, milk and vanilla pod in the top pan, cover and simmer for about 1 hour, stirring from time to time and replenishing the water in the bottom pan if necessary. The rice should have absorbed all the milk and look like a creamy mush, speckled with tiny particles from the vanilla pod. Remove the pod and stir in the sugar and coconut. When partly cooled, add the rum and sour cream. Chill until needed.
● Before serving pour the rice pudding into a dish with the drained lychees.

Serves 6

Pear Sorbet with Poached Pears

Uncooked pears are used for the sorbet to contrast with the poached ones which accompany it. Sorbets are at their best when eaten within 24 hours. Serve this delicate pudding to end a rather rich meal.

— *Pear Sorbet* —

½ pt (250 ml) water

12 oz (350 g) sugar

5 pears

juice of 2 lemons

2 tablespoons pear eau-de-vie

2 egg whites

a few fresh mint sprigs

— *Poached Pears* —

½ pt (250 ml) red wine

½ pt (250 ml) water

4 oz (125 g) sugar

6 pears

● For the sorbet, gently heat the water and sugar. Remove from heat when the syrup starts boiling. Allow to cool.
● In a blender or food processor, reduce the peeled and cored pears to a pulp with the lemon juice. Mix with the syrup. Lastly stir in the pear eau-de-vie. Pour the mixture into a metal tray and freeze for 2–3 hours or until mushy (crystals will have formed). Beat the mixture again until frothy. Beat the egg whites until they form soft peaks. Fold into the pear mixture and freeze until firm.
● For the poached pears, prepare a syrup with the wine, water and sugar. Peel, quarter and core the pears and drop them into the syrup. Simmer until the fruit is soft but not flabby – about 8 minutes. Allow to cool in the syrup until needed. Cut each quarter into 5 slices.
● An hour before serving, transfer the sorbet to the refrigerator. Scoop it out. Serve with the poached pears and a sprig of mint for decoration.

Serves 8

Clockwise from top: *Health Drink (p.119), Pear Sorbet with Poached Pears, Rice and Coconut Pudding with Lychees*

Orange Curd in Tangerine Shells

For this recipe, buy tangerines with loose skins, to make peeling easier. The discarded segments can be used in a watercress or spinach salad. If you like, freeze the pudding – shell and all – and serve with Aniseed Biscuits, p. 116. You can replace the orange flower water with Grand Marnier for a more grown-up version.

6 tangerines

2 large oranges

3 eggs, lightly beaten

2 oz (60 g) caster sugar

2 teaspoons orange flower water

4 oz (125 g) unsalted butter

¼ pt/5 fl oz (150 ml) whipping or double cream

• Cut off a lid of skin from each tangerine. With a small spoon, gently loosen the segments from the skin and remove them through the hole, without damaging the skin which you will use as a container.
• Grate the zest from the oranges, then squeeze the juice. Put the orange zest and juice, the eggs, sugar and orange flower water in the top of a double-boiler. Make sure the boiling water is not in contact with the bottom of the basin. Whisk all the ingredients until thick. Remove from the heat, allow to cool a little and add the butter (which should be soft, but not melted) bit by bit. Half whip the cream and fold into the thoroughly cooled mixture. Divide the curd equally among the tangerine shells and replace the lids on top. Chill or freeze, depending on the way you wish to serve this pudding.

Serves 6

Pomegranate and Orange Salad with Ginger

This simple fruit salad looks very festive with its dazzling, translucent colours. The sharpness of the pomegranate and orange counteracts the luscious texture and spicy flavour of crystallized ginger. This looks particularly beautiful made with blood oranges, which give it a slightly less sharp flavour.

2 pomegranates

5 oranges

3 pieces crystallized ginger

a few dashes Angostura bitters

1 tablespoon caster sugar (optional)

• Peel the pomegranates, then carefully remove the white membranes, taking care not to break the juice-laden seeds. Separate the seeds and reserve with the juice.
• Peel the oranges, also removing the transparent skin, catching the juice in a bowl. Slice thinly, removing the pips and white pith. If desired, cut the slices in two. Add these, with the juice, to the pomegranates.
• Cut the ginger into paper-thin slices. Scatter them over the fruit and add a few dashes of Angostura bitters and a little sugar if you like. Toss gently and serve in a glass dish or bowl.

Serves 6

Top: *Orange Curd in Tangerine Shells*
Bottom: *Pomegranate and Orange Salad with Ginger*

110

Frozen White Chocolate Mousse with Almond Jelly

This is a white-on-white pudding. The almond jelly is an idea from Vietnamese cookery, where it is served with lychees, but here it accompanies chocolate. The flavours nicely complement each other.

---

1 packet (½ oz/12 g) gelatine

¾ pt (450 ml) water

¼ pt/5 fl oz (150 ml) full-cream milk or single cream

1½ tablespoons caster sugar

½ teaspoon almond essence

7 oz (200 g) white chocolate

4 oz (125 g) caster sugar

¾ pt/15 fl oz (450 ml) double cream, lightly whipped

● First make the almond jelly: lightly oil a 6 × 6 in (15 × 15 cm) ice tray. Sprinkle the gelatine into a bowl containing 2 tablespoons of cold water. Place the bowl over a pan of very hot water. Stir until dissolved.
● In another saucepan, heat the ½ pint (300 ml) water with the milk (or cream), 1½ tablespoons of sugar and the almond essence. Stir until the sugar is completely dissolved. Then add the gelatine and pour into the tray. Let it cool and chill until set. (When set, the jelly might have separated so that it is clear on the bottom and opaque on top. This is perfectly all right.)
● Put the chocolate, broken into pieces, and ¼ pint (150 ml) water into a heavy saucepan. Heat until the chocolate has melted and add 4 oz (125 g) of sugar. Reduce, cooking the mixture a further 10–12 minutes, stirring constantly with a wooden spoon. Cool. When cold, fold in the whipped cream carefully. Pour the mixture into six individual ramequins. Freeze for 3 hours.
● Serve as is, or run a knife blade around the sides of the ramequins, invert and, giving a shake, unmould onto a pretty dish. Cut the almond jelly into diamond shapes and arrange on the dish. If you like, decorate with extra grated chocolate. Serve immediately.

Serves 6

Sugared Pasta with Praline

This unusual pudding is made with tagliatelle. Do not be put off by the idea, as it tastes delicious.

---

4 oz (125 g) caster sugar

4 tablespoons water

4 oz (125 g) hazelnuts, finely chopped

1 lb (500 g) green tagliatelle (or 1½ lb/750 g if fresh)

2 tablespoons hazelnut oil

1 heaped tablespoon granulated sugar

a few gratings of nutmeg

● First make the praline: in a heavy saucepan, melt the sugar in the water until the sugar turns a light brown colour. Stir in the nuts and pour onto a greased surface. Allow to cool and harden, then break into small pieces. Reduce to a crumble in a food processor.
● Fill a saucepan three-quarters full of water and bring to the boil. Cook the tagliatelle for 8–10 minutes if dried, or 40 seconds if fresh. Drain, and put in a bowl. Toss in the oil and granulated sugar. Allow to cool. Transfer to a flat dish and, just before serving, sprinkle with the praline and a little nutmeg.

Serves 6–8

Left: *Frozen White Chocolate Mousse with Almond Jelly* Right: *Sugared Pasta with Praline*

Caramelized Plums

Use large plums for this dish; Victoria plums are ideal. If you like, serve with Japanese Sorbet, p.107, which is made with plum wine, and with almond biscuits or small macaroons.

2 lb (1 kg) large plums

a little oil, a light one such as sunflower

½ lb (250 g) caster sugar

½ teaspoon ground cinnamon or allspice

● Wipe the plums, cut them in two lengthways and stone them. Place them, cut side down, on a pretty flameproof dish. Brush the skins lightly with oil. Mix the sugar and cinnamon thoroughly and sprinkle over the plums (the oil will ensure that the sugar mixture sticks to the fruits). Grill for a few minutes or until caramelized. Allow to cool, and serve.

Serves 6

Semi-Frozen Yoghurt with Blueberries

This delicate and light dessert is not quite an ice cream. The yoghurt contrasts nicely with the blueberries.

1 packet (½ oz/12 g) gelatine

2 tablespoons cold water

3 tablespoons clear honey, such as acacia

¼ teaspoon vanilla essence

¾ pt/15 fl oz (450 ml) Greek yoghurt, at room temperature

1 lb (500 g) fresh blueberries

● In a small bowl, sprinkle the gelatine over the cold water. Leave for a few minutes or until swollen. Place the bowl over a pan of barely simmering water and stir until completely dissolved. Leave over the water, off the heat.
● Beat the honey in a bowl with the vanilla essence and add the yoghurt. Then stir in the gelatine. Pour the mixture into a metal container and freeze for 3 hours (the partly frozen yoghurt should still be soft in texture).
● Serve the semi-frozen yoghurt with the blueberries scattered on the top.

Serves 6–8

Variation: Wash 2 lb (1 kg) damsons and put them in an enamelled saucepan with just enough water to cover the bottom. Heat, then simmer for 15–20 minutes, adding ½ lb (250 g) of sugar halfway through. Allow to cool. Serve with the yoghurt.

Left: *Semi-Frozen Yoghurt with Blueberries*
Right: *Caramelized Plums*

Apple and Poppy Seed Cake

This is a cake to serve, lavishly buttered, at teatime. It improves if kept a day before eating, but do not keep it longer than five days.

---

8 oz (250 g) butter, plus extra for greasing

8 oz (250 g) demerara sugar

3 large eggs

14 oz (400 g) plain flour

3 teaspoons baking powder

¼ pt/5 fl oz (150 ml) milk

5 tablespoons poppy seeds

grated rind of 1 lemon

3 apples, such as russets, peeled, cored and sliced

● Preheat the oven to 350°F/180°C/Gas 4. Grease with butter, line with greaseproof paper and grease again a cake tin measuring about 5 × 8 in (12 × 20 cm). Cream the butter and sugar until light and a rich yellow colour, then add the eggs one by one, beating well between additions.
● Sift the flour with the baking powder and stir it into the butter mixture alternately with the milk. The consistency should be fairly stiff. Lastly stir in the poppy seeds, lemon rind and slices of 2 apples.
● Transfer the mixture to the prepared tin, placing the remaining apple slices overlapping in rows on top. With the back of a spoon, push them in until barely buried. Bake for 1½ hours, or until a skewer inserted in the centre comes out clean and the cake has shrunk a little from the sides of the tin. After 1 hour check the cake and, if it is getting too brown, cover loosely with a piece of foil.
● When ready, allow the cake to cool in the tin for 15 minutes before turning it out onto a rack.

Makes a 2½lb (1.25 kg) cake

Aniseed Biscuits

These are thin, brittle biscuits. If you like, you can sandwich them together with a little raspberry jam spread in the centre.

---

8 oz (250 g) plain flour

3 oz (90 g) caster sugar, plus a little extra

2½ teaspoons whole aniseed

½ teaspoon ground cinnamon

3 oz (100 g) butter at room temperature, plus extra for greasing

1 egg yolk

● Preheat the oven to 350°F/180°C/Gas 4. Butter two oven trays and line them with buttered greaseproof paper.
● Stir together the flour, sugar, aniseed and cinnamon, and rub in the butter. Mix the egg yolk with a little water and add to the other ingredients to make a smooth dough. Roll out thinly and use a wavy-edged biscuit cutter to make circles about 1¼in (3 cm) in diameter. Place on the prepared trays and bake for 12 minutes. Sprinkle with extra sugar and lift carefully with a spatula on to a wire rack to cool.

Makes about 25 biscuits

Left: *Apple and Poppy Seed Cake*
Right: *Aniseed Biscuits*

Cardamom and Orange Cake

As this is a spicy cake, its flavour will improve if it is kept three days before eating. It should keep well for over a week. If you like, serve it with plenty of butter and jam at teatime, or with stewed fruits at the end of a meal.

---

4 oz (125 g) butter, at room temperature, plus more for greasing

8 oz (250 g) caster sugar, plus 2 extra tablespoons

2 large eggs

grated rind and juice of 2 oranges, about ¼ pt (150 ml)

8 oz (250 g) plain flour

2 teaspoons baking powder

a pinch of salt

seeds from 12–15 cardamom pods, lightly crushed

● Preheat the oven to 350°F/180°C/Gas 4. Line and grease with butter a 10 in (25 cm) deep circular cake tin or loaf tin.
● Cream the butter and 8 oz (250 g) sugar and work in the eggs, orange rind and juice. Sift the flour, baking powder and salt together and fold into the butter and sugar mixture. Finally add the cardamom seeds. Pour the batter into the prepared tin and sprinkle the remaining sugar on top.
● Bake the cake for 1¼ hours. Allow to cool for 10 minutes in the tin, and then transfer onto a wire rack until cool.

Makes a 1½ lb (750 g) cake

Clockwise from left: *Cardamom and Orange Cake, Rampon, Tiramisu (p.120)*

Rampon

I first discovered this drink on an island in Chile. I couldn't find out the origin of the name but I know that it is a very deceptive drink, as its sweetness somehow diminishes your awareness of the rum.

---

14 oz (400 g) tin condensed milk

2 egg yolks

¼ teaspoon vanilla essence

¾ pt (450 ml) white rum

crushed ice

● Put all the ingredients in a blender and mix for 1 minute. Pour into a bottle, cork and keep refrigerated until needed. Serve chilled in tall glasses filled with crushed ice.

Makes about 1¼ pints (750 ml)

Health Drink

This is a rich, fragrant drink with a lovely velvety texture. I often make it to replace lunch, when in a hurry. It will immediately restore sagging energy. Serve with wholemeal scones or Saffron Bread, p.17.

---

1 avocado, peeled and stoned

about 6 strawberries

juice of 1 orange

a sprig of fresh mint for decoration

● Put all the ingredients in a blender and whizz for 1 minute or until thoroughly blended and mousse-like. Pour into a tall glass and drop a mint sprig on top.

Serves 1

Chocolate Shell Cakes

These are similar to the French madeleine cakes, with their light, melt-in-the-mouth, airy texture. I use scallop shells as moulds, so you might ask your fishmonger to save you a dozen of them. The combination of chocolate and nutmeg gives an intriguing, lingering flavour to the cakes. Serve with ice cream, with coffee or at teatime.

---

8 oz (250 g) butter, plus some for greasing

6 oz (175 g) bitter chocolate

6 oz (175 g) plain flour

1 scant teaspoon grated nutmeg

6 large eggs

8 oz (250 g) granulated sugar

1 tablespoon icing sugar

● Preheat the oven to 375°F/190°C/Gas 5.
● Grease generously about twenty scallop shells (maybe less will be needed, depending on their size). In a double boiler set over a pan of barely simming water, melt the butter and chocolate. Remove the mixture from the heat and allow to cool.
● Meanwhile, sift the flour and nutmeg together. In a bowl, beat the eggs and sugar together until thickened and a pale straw colour. Incorporate, alternately, some of the flour then some of the chocolate mixture, folding gently after each addition until it is just combined.
● Divide the batter evenly among the prepared shells, not quite reaching the rims to avoid the mixture spilling over when baking. Pile up the batter higher on the hinge ends to simulate the true shell shape. Then smooth over the tops with the back of a metal spoon.
● Place the shells on metal biscuit cutters or individual moulds so that they are standing straight on the oven tray. Bake for 25–30 minutes or until a skewer inserted in the centre comes out clean. Carefully invert the cakes onto

a wire rack and allow to cool.
● Sift the icing sugar into a small bowl. Sprinkle over the ribbed side of the cakes, and rub in gently with the tips of your fingers so that the shell-shaped cakes have a textured appearance.

Makes about 20 cakes

Tiramisu

This is an Italian cake literally meaning 'pull me up' (probably needed after eating this luscious, rich dessert). Tiramisu is a roulade, moistened with spirit, and with a mascarpone filling (an Italian equivalent of cream cheese). This cake would improve if left refrigerated overnight, thus allowing the flavours to mingle and mature.

---

oil for greasing

5 eggs, separated

4 oz (100 g) caster sugar

4 oz (100 g) plain flour

7 tablespoons rum or kirsch

icing sugar for dusting

--- *Filling* ---

1½ lb (750 g) mascarpone or cream cheese

2 tablespoons rum or kirsch

3 oz (75 g) caster sugar

2 teaspoons cocoa powder

● Preheat the oven to 425°F/220°C/Gas 7. Line a 9 × 13 in (23 × 33 cm) Swiss roll tin with greaseproof paper. Brush lightly with oil and pinch the paper at the four corners to keep the edges upright. Beat the egg yolks and caster sugar until fluffy and a pale straw colour. Whisk the egg whites to soft peaks. Fold a quarter of the beaten whites into the yolk mixture to lighten it. Then fold the remaining egg whites in gently with a spatula or large metal spoon, taking care not to overmix. Pour evenly onto the prepared tin. Spread, if necessary, with the back of a spoon, breaking any large mounds of egg white.

● Bake for 15 minutes or until firm but springy to the touch. Let it cool for a few minutes. Place a large clean piece of lightly-oiled foil over the roulade. Turn over carefully, holding the baking tin on top to make the task easier. Then peel off the paper. Moisten with the rum and cut across into three layers.

● To make the filling: in a bowl, mash the mascarpone (or cream cheese) with the rum (or kirsch), the sugar and the cocoa powder, until the mixture is well blended.

● Spread half the filling over the first layer and level on top. Place the second layer on the filling and repeat the operation once again. Finally, place the last layer on top and wrap tightly with the foil paper, pinching the edges. Refrigerate for at least 3 hours or, better, overnight. Before serving, dust with icing sugar.

Serves 6–8

Clerico

This is a Uruguayan drink which is served on hot summer days. It would be a good idea to leave the fruits to steep into the white wine for an hour or so before drinking. Replenish with more chilled wine two or three times before replacing the fruits. Serve with meals al fresco.

---

2 apples, one red, one green

2 oranges

2 nectarines or peaches

2 bananas (optional)

2–3 sprigs fresh mint

1 bottle dry white wine, chilled

● Cut the apples and core them, without peeling. Then cut again into large chunks. Peel and slice the orange, removing pith and pips. Cut, stone and quarter the nectarines (or peaches). Peel and slice the bananas if used.

● Place all the prepared fruits, along with the mint sprigs, in a jug. Pour on the wine and chill until needed.

Makes about 2 pints (1.2 litres)

Apricot and Oat Slices

The combination of wholemeal flour and oats gives this dish a nutty flavour which marries well with the apricot's slight tartness. Serve with a jug of sour cream.

---

1 lb (500 g) apricots

8 oz (250 g) butter

4 oz (125 g) demerara sugar

11 oz (375 g) wholemeal flour

6 oz (175 g) rolled oats

a pinch of salt

● Preheat the oven to 350°F/180°C/Gas 4. Halve and stone the apricots. Break the stones to extract the kernels. Peel the kernels and split in two. Place fruit and kernels in an enamel saucepan with 2 tablespoons of water. Cover and simmer until nearly reduced to a purée. Allow to cool.

● Meanwhile, melt the butter and sugar together. Take off the heat and add the flour, oats and salt. Stir in the apricot purée.

● Press the mixture down into a rectangular tin about 11 × 7 in (27.5 × 17.5 cm). Bake for 30 minutes.

● Allow to cool and serve sliced. (Be careful as the slices are rather crumbly.)

Serves 6–8

Marzipan, Coffee and Walnut Bundle

This white marzipan bundle is spotted with brown instant coffee granules. Concealed inside is a cream cheese and walnut filling. Give it to friends as a present, or serve with coffee or at teatime.

---

1 lb (500 g) white marzipan

2 tablespoons instant coffee granules

8 fresh walnuts, shelled

½ lb (250 g) cream cheese

● Roll out the marzipan into a square about 8 × 8 in (20 × 20 cm). (To prevent the marzipan from sticking, roll it out between two large pieces of greaseproof paper.) Lift the square gently, sprinkle the coffee granules evenly on a work surface, and place the marzipan on top Press gently, so that the coffee sticks to it.
● Break the walnuts into smallish pieces, and mash them into the cream cheese. Shape into a mound and place this in the centre of the marzipan. Gather the four corners of the square and pinch halfway down, thus making a bundle. Fold the points in a pretty fashion.

Serves 6

Variation: Cut the marzipan into small squares and divide the filling between them to make individual bundles. You will need a smaller overall quantity of filling.

From left to right: *Marzipan, Coffee and Walnut Bundle, Chocolate Shell Cakes (p. 120), Clerico (p. 121)*

Coconut and Orange Muffins

I serve these at teatime, often lavishly spread with lemon curd. They are also nice accompanying a fruit salad with orange or red fruits.

---

8 oz (250 g) plain flour

3 oz (90 g) sugar

1 heaped tablespoon baking powder

2 eggs, lightly beaten

4 oz (125 g) butter, melted, plus more to grease moulds

about ¼ pt/5 fl oz (150 ml) yoghurt

2 oz (60 g) unsweetened desiccated coconut

grated zest and juice of 1 orange

● Preheat the oven to 375°F/190°C/Gas 5. Butter twelve muffin cups generously. In a large bowl, sift together flour, sugar and baking powder. In another bowl stir the eggs, cooled butter, yoghurt, coconut and orange zest and juice together with a wooden spoon until the mixture is well blended. (The yoghurt and orange juice should make up 8 fl oz (250 ml) of liquid, so use only part of the yoghurt, adding a little milk later if the batter is too stiff.)

● Stir the egg mixture into the flour mixture until they are just combined. The batter should be lumpy. Fill the muffin cups three-quarters full and bake for 25 minutes, or until a skewer inserted in the centres comes out clean. Remove from the oven and turn out onto a cake rack. Leave to cool.

Makes 12 muffins

Left: *Apricot and Oat Slices (p.120)*
Right: *Coconut and Orange Muffins*

INDEX

Page numbers in *italic* refer to the illustrations. *indicates vegetarian recipes.